INTO THE CLA

RELIGIOUS EDUCATION IN THE LEAVING CERTIFICATE

Worship, Prayer and Ritual

Christopher O'Donnell, OCarm

Series Editors
Eoin G. Cassidy and Patrick M. Devitt

VERITAS

First published 2004 by
Veritas Publications
7/8 Lower Abbey Street
Dublin 1
Ireland
Email publications@veritas.ie
Website www.veritas.ie

ISBN 1 85390 776 6

10 9 8 7 6 5 4 3 2 1

A catalogue record for this book is available from the British Library.

Cover design by Bill Bolger
Printed in the Republic of Ireland by Betaprint Ltd, Dublin

*Veritas books are printed on paper made from the wood pulp of managed
forests. For every tree felled, at least one tree is planted, thereby renewing
natural resources.*

Contents

Series Introduction

September 2003 saw the introduction of the Leaving Certificate Religious Education Syllabus by the Department of Education and Science. For those concerned to promote a religious sensibility in young Irish adults it is hard to exaggerate the importance of this event. It both represents a formal recognition by society of the value of religious education in the academic lives of second-level students, and it also reflects the importance which Irish society attaches to promoting the personal growth of students, including their spiritual and moral development. Religious education offers young people the opportunity to understand and interpret their experience in the light of a religious world-view. Furthermore, in and through an engagement with the RE Syllabus at Leaving Certificate level, students will learn a language that will enable them both to articulate their own faith experience and to dialogue with those of different faiths or non-theistic stances.

The Department of Education Syllabus is to be welcomed in that it gives recognition to the role that religious education plays in the human development of the young person. It is not an exaggeration to say that religious education is the capstone of the school's educational response to the young person's search for meaning and values. In this context, it encourages students to reflect upon their awareness of themselves as unique individuals with roots in a community network of family, friends and parish. Furthermore, it allows students to acknowledge and reflect upon their relationship to a God who cares for them and for the world in which we live. Finally, it gives students access to the universal nature of the quest for truth, beauty and goodness. Most of these themes are addressed sympathetically in the section entitled *The Search for Meaning and Values*. In particular, this section is to be welcomed because it offers the possibility for students to grapple with theistic and non-theistic world-views in a context that is hospitable to religious belief.

A critical dimension of the young person's educational journey is the growth in understanding of their own culture and the manner in which culture shapes their outlook on the world. The Religious Education Syllabus not only addresses the manner in which religion (and in particular Christianity) has shaped Irish culture over many centuries, but it also provides an extremely valuable platform from which to critique aspects of the relationship between faith and culture in the contemporary world. The section entitled *Religion: The Irish Experience* addresses the former concern by showing pupils the manner in which the Christian religion has contributed to the belief patterns and values of Irish society. It also alerts them to the depths of religious belief that predate by many centuries, even millennia, the arrival of Christianity in Ireland; and it also connects them to the cultural richness that links Ireland to the European continent. In this context, the devotional revolution that took place in Ireland (including the extraordinary growth in religious orders from 1850-1930) is a topic that could be expanded. The missionary outreach of the Catholic Church in Ireland in the last hundred years is worthy of special mention. Finally, students studying this section should be encouraged to acknowledge the ambiguities that have attended the presence of religion in Ireland over the centuries; to see on the one hand the image of an island of saints and scholars, and on the other hand to note how 'lilies that fester smell far worse than weeds'.

In examining the manner in which faith and culture interact, the sections entitled *Religion and Science* and *Religion and Gender* make a valuable contribution to the Syllabus. These sections address topical issues that were controversial in the past and continue to be problematical even today. In treating of these two topics it is obviously important to avoid stereotypes – the acceptance of unexamined assumptions that mask or over-simplify the truth to such an extent as to do a disservice to the seriousness of the issues involved. Likewise, the section on *World Religions* should be taught in a manner that is sensitive to the dangers of cultural and religious stereotypes. This section not only gives students a valuable introduction to the main religions in the world, but it also provides a cultural context for an awareness of the fact that the phenomenon of religion and the experience of religious belief is something that shapes people's understanding of themselves and their lifestyles across all cultural boundaries. Furthermore, it should never be forgotten that if, as Christians believe, God's Spirit is present in and through these religions, there is a need to study these religions precisely in order to discover aspects of God's presence in the world that has the capability to continually surprise.

In the Irish cultural context, Catholicism shapes the religious sensibilities and practices of the majority of young people. The Syllabus offers a generous acknowledgement of the importance of Christianity in the Irish context by providing two sections that focus on core aspects of the Christian faith. These are: *Christianity: origins and contemporary expressions* and *The Bible: Literature and Sacred text.* In this context, the Syllabus section on the Bible is to be welcomed. However, greater attention could be given to the role and significance of the Prophets in the Old Testament and to Paul in the New Testament. Furthermore, in studying the Bible it should never be forgotten that the primary reality is not the 'book' but rather the person of Christ and the community tradition grappling with this reality that is revealed in and through the Bible.

What is often in danger of being forgotten in an academic context is the importance of the fostering of attitudes and practices that promote personal growth. Religious education cannot be focused only on knowledge and understanding, because religion is primarily a way of celebrating life and, in particular, the spiritual dimension of life in and through the practices of worship, ritual and prayer. The Syllabus's recognition of this critical dimension of religious education through the section entitled *Worship, Ritual and Prayer* is to be welcomed. In addressing this section of the Syllabus it would be important to alert students to the great variety of spiritualities, prayer forms, mysticisms, rituals and styles of music that are to be found within the Christian tradition in order that students may have the possibility of exploring the richness of the spiritual dimension of their own tradition.

A key remit of the educational process is the fostering of moral maturity through a syllabus that allows students to engage in moral education. Not only is religious education particularly suited to facilitating this educational imperative, but the ethical character of human life is a core feature of all religions. The importance of this dimension of religious education is recognised in the provision of two sections entitled *Moral Decision Making* and *Issues of Justice and Peace*. There is nothing optional about the challenge to promote justice and peace. However, it is a topic that can all too easily be ideologically driven. Therefore, there is a special responsibility on those teaching this section to ensure that the instances of injustice cited, and the causes of injustice proposed, are grounded in solid research.

The challenges to Catholic religion teachers
Though religious education has been an integral part of Irish second-level schools long before the foundation of the state, it

has not until now been possible to assess this work under the State examination system. The reason for this anomaly is the Intermediate Education Act (1878) which allowed for the teaching but forbade the State examination of religious education. The removal of this legal constraint on State examination of RE has provided the impetus for the introduction of the Junior Certificate Syllabus in September 2000 and the introduction of the Leaving Certificate Syllabus in September 2003. These changes are to be welcomed but they provide a number of major challenges to Catholic religion teachers that should not be minimised.

In the *first* place, Catholic religion teachers have to attend to the danger that the new Syllabus will lead to a weakening of a commitment to catechesis in second level schools. The catechetical project of faith formation is built around six key pillars: knowledge of the faith; liturgical/sacramental education; moral formation; learning to pray; education for community life, including a fostering of the ecumenical character of Christian community, and finally, missionary initiative and inter-religious dialogue. Clearly, the RE Leaving Certificate Syllabus does give attention to many of the above themes, including the key catechetical concerns of attitude or value formation and the development of commitments. However, the emphasis in the Syllabus is undoubtedly upon the acquiring of knowledge, understanding and knowledge-based skills, all of which undoubtedly place it under the rubric of religious education rather than catechesis. The religion teacher ought to value the distinctive approaches to religion reflected in both catechesis and religious education. Both are important because both contribute in distinctive ways to the religious development of the young person. Catechesis aims at maturity of faith whereas religious education aims at knowledge and understanding of the faith.

From the point of view of the religion teacher, the teaching can have a different tone at different times. On one occasion, it might have a 'showing how' or catechetical tone, one that assumes a shared faith experience and encourages active participation. At another time it can have an educational or 'explaining' tone that invites pupils to stand back from religion to a certain extent, so that they can gain a more objective understanding of what is being taught. The Religious Education Syllabus should be taught in a manner that keeps both of these approaches in balance. In a similar vein, the presence of RE on the Leaving Certificate curriculum should not distract teachers from acknowledging that the religious development of young people happens in many contexts, which are distinct, though complementary. It can take place at home, in the parish, with friends as well as in school. Furthermore, even in the school it can take place at a whole series of levels including liturgy, prayer and projects that encourage an awareness of the need to care for those in most need.

In the *second* place, teachers have to attend to the scope and range of the aims of the Syllabus, one that seeks both to introduce students to a broad range of religious traditions and to the non-religious interpretation of life as well as providing students with the opportunity to develop an informed and critical understanding of the Christian tradition. In this context, teachers have to balance the need to promote tolerance for and mutual understanding of those of other or no religious traditions, alongside the need to give explicit attention to the Christian faith claims that Jesus is the Son of God and that he died to save us and to unite us with God and one another. Similarly, in teaching Christianity, teachers need to give attention to the role and significance of the Church from a Catholic perspective. It should never be forgotten that the idea of the Church as 'people of God', 'body of Christ' and 'temple of the Holy Spirit' is one that is at the heart of Catholic self-understanding.

In a similar vein, the Syllabus encourages students to engage critically with a wide variety of ethical codes with a view to the development of a moral maturity. Teachers will have to balance this approach with the way in which morality is viewed within the Christian tradition under the heading of discipleship – Jesus invites people to follow *him* rather than an ethical code or vision. Furthermore, from a Christian perspective, morality is never simply or even primarily concerned with a listing of moral prohibitions, rather it situates the ethical dimension of human nature within the context of a belief in a forgiving God. Finally, it should not be forgotten that it does not make sense to teach morality in too abstract a manner. Morality is something preeminently practical and at all times needs to be brought down to the level of real people – those who struggle with the demands of conscience in their lives. From a Catholic perspective, one has in the lives of the saints a multitude of examples of the manner in which people have attempted to follow the call to discipleship that is Christian morality.

Finally, nobody concerned with the seriousness of the challenge facing schools to promote moral maturity could be unaware of the importance of the contemporary challenge posed to the promotion of societal and religious values by the rise of a relativist and/or subjectivist ethos. In this context, the teaching of the broad variety of moral codes will have to be done in a manner that draws students' attention to the importance of acknowledging the objective nature of morality as opposed to accepting uncritically either a relativist or a subjectivist standpoint. In the light of the need to critique an exaggerated acceptance of pluralism, there is also a need to acknowledge that not all theories are equally valid, and moral decision-making is not simply a matter of applying one's own personal preference.

What is proposed in these commentaries

Given the breadth and scope of the Syllabus it is undoubtedly true that teachers will have to attend to the wide variety of sections in the Syllabus which demand a breadth of knowledge that some may find a little daunting. Even though it is not envisaged that teachers would attempt to teach all ten sections of the Syllabus to any one group of students, nevertheless, the Syllabus will make demands upon teachers that can only be met if there are support services in place. For example, apart from the need to ensure the publishing of good quality teaching and learning resources, the schools themselves will need to ensure that appropriate resources – books, CDs, internet and videos – are provided. Finally, teachers will need to be provided with appropriate in-service training. It is to furthering this goal of providing good quality teaching and learning resources that the present series of volumes is addressed.

The eleven volumes in this series of commentaries comprise an introductory volume (already published, *Willingly To School*) that reflects upon the challenge of RE as an examination subject, along with ten other volumes that mirror the ten sections in the Syllabus. These commentaries on the Syllabus have been published to address the critical issue of the need to provide resources for the teaching of the Syllabus that are both academically rigorous and yet accessible to the educated general reader. Although primarily addressed to both specialist and general teachers of religion and third-level students studying to be religion teachers, the commentaries will be accessible to parents of Leaving Certificate pupils and, in addition, it is to be hoped that they will provide an important focus for adults in parish-based or other religious education or theology programmes. In the light of this focus, each of the volumes is structured in order to closely reflect the content of the Syllabus and its order of presentation. Furthermore, they are written in clear, easily accessible language and each includes an explanation of new theological and philosophical perspectives.

The volumes offered in this series are as follows

Patrick M. Devitt:	*Willingly to School: Religious Education as an Examination Subject*
Eoin G. Cassidy:	*The Search for Meaning and Values*
Thomas Norris and Brendan Leahy:	*Christianity: Origins and Contemporary Expressions*
Philip Barnes:	*World Religions*
Patrick Hannon:	*Moral Decision Making*
Sandra Cullen:	*Religion and Gender*
John Murray:	*Issues of Justice and Peace*
Christopher O'Donnell:	*Worship, Prayer and Ritual*
Benedict Hegarty:	*The Bible: Literature and Sacred Text*
John Walsh:	*Religion: The Irish Experience*
Fachtna McCarthy and Joseph McCann:	*Religion and Science*

Thanks are due to the generosity of our contributors who so readily agreed to write a commentary on each of the sections in the new Leaving Certificate Syllabus. Each of them brings to their commentary both academic expertise and a wealth of experience in the teaching of their particular area. In the light of this, one should not underestimate the contribution that they will make to the work of preparing teachers for this challenging project. Thanks are also due to our publishers, Veritas. Their unfailing encouragement and practical support has been of inestimable value to us and has ensured that these volumes saw the light of day. Finally, we hope that you the reader will find each of these commentaries helpful as you negotiate the paths of a new and challenging syllabus.

Eoin G. Cassidy
Patrick M. Devitt
Series Editors

Preface

I have enjoyed writing this book and so I am very grateful to Drs Eoin Cassidy and Patrick Devitt for their invitation to work on it. The splendid part of the new Syllabus on Worship, Prayer and Ritual (Section G) led me into areas that both taught and stimulated me greatly. I hope that teachers also will take pleasure in presenting this very challenging section to their students. Parents will hopefully be helped by a commentary on the material that their children are studying.

The Syllabus allows much choice in the illustrations and parallels to be studied. Given the situation in Ireland, especially the North, I gave more prominence to the Church of Ireland for comparative studies of other Christians. As this work was nearing completion, the Church of Ireland issued its impressive revision of *The Book of Common Prayer*. It was possible to utilise it in several chapters. We should surely congratulate the Church on this fine achievement. It is the fruit of many years work. It shows that compromise and comprehensiveness can be positive gifts, marking Anglican life at its best.

In the case of other religions I focused on Islam, the religion of a growing number of immigrants who are coming to Ireland. A consideration of its spiritual life and especially its prayer can help people to gain a new respect for a great and beautiful world religion.

The fact that the author of this volume is Roman Catholic will be obvious to readers, but hopefully not in a way offensive to other Christian believers or members of other faiths. It is possible, one hopes, to have great openness and appreciation of other beliefs, without agreeing that all religions are the same or that it does not matter what one believes in, so long as one has active faith and good moral standards.

With some hesitation I have added reading suggestions at the end of each chapter. There is so much written on the subject matter of this volume that many valuable books must go unmentioned. The recommendation of particular titles does not imply that it is necessarily the best on the topic of the chapter. As the new Syllabus gets into swing, more and more helpful books will be noted, recommended and eventually written on its topics. I refer continually to two rather expensive reference books that may be available in libraries, *The New Dictionary of Spirituality* and *The New Dictionary of Sacramental Theology*. These are outstanding for the clarity and authority of their entries and for the short bibliographies.

I have been greatly helped by several people. I mention again the series editors who were extremely patient as one deadline after another slipped. Patrick Devitt was a careful and encouraging reader of the text. For matters of the Church of Ireland I have been greatly helped by the Reverend Kevin Moroney of the Church of Ireland Theological College, Dublin 14. I received generous and valuable advice from Mr Mustafidh Gani at The Islamic Cultural Centre, Dublin 14. I owe special thanks to Mary Carroll, religious education teacher and member of the chaplaincy team at Terenure College. As finishing this book seemed to become ever more problematic, I had the support and prayers of many friends. Finally, I again experienced the truth that behind any half-middling book one finds a good copy editor. So my thanks to Toner Quinn, and to Helen Carr of Veritas Publications.

I dedicate this work to religious educators, especially those who will be taking up the challenge of the new Syllabus.

Christopher O'Donnell, OCarm
Milltown Institute of Theology and Philosophy
Dublin 6

Carmelite Institute,
Rome

Part One

SYMBOL, RITUAL AND SACRAMENT

I

Symbol

Symbols are so much part of us that human life as we know it would be impossible without them. It is, however, one thing to move comfortably in a world of symbols, it is something quite else to try to grasp them and perceive how they operate. In the past few decades there has been much study of symbols, which can help us to understand ourselves and our world. But there is not full agreement about symbols by all the many kinds of people who analyse or theorise about them: philosophers, psychologists, anthropologists, operatives in marketing, artists, workers in the media, religious thinkers and many others. Hence, though it is possible to speak about symbols in a way that might be generally acceptable, on particular issues authors and experts will differ on many areas of interpretation and in the language they use. This problem of interpretation is particularly marked in the religious field. Religious symbols are a special class, which, however, share many of the characteristics of all symbols. One could begin by attempting to heighten one's awareness of symbols generally in our world.

Secular symbols

A moment's thought will show how widespread symbols are in our lives. We use them because we are corporeal beings with mind, feelings, desires and imagination. Symbols are all around us: uniforms, traffic indications, directions and instructions are usually symbolic as well as practical. Advertising depends largely on symbols. Sometimes when we see a TV advertisement for the first time, we may not know until the end what product or service is being advertised; sometimes it is unmistakable from the outset. Advertising operates on our imagination, on our feelings and to some extent on our reason to evoke a desire such as to purchase some item, to participate in some group or to avail of a service. The immediate appeal of an advertisement may be direct, as when we are shown condensation bubbles on a glass or can to suggest a cool, refreshing drink. It may seek to suggest to us that some product will change our lives, or attractiveness, our potential; sexuality is often used in such advertisements. An important example of symbols on which millions of euro are spent is logotype, commonly called a logo, which is an artificial word or set of letters, usually incorporating a design which sets apart a business firm, a team, an institution, an organisation, or some group and makes them readily identifiable. Firms are very protective of their logos; it is a major and expensive decision to change them. It can also be risky, as the new logo may not work as well as the old. A logo is a particular kind of symbol.

The world of symbols is a rich and complex one. The word itself is from Greek, *symbolon* meaning a token, itself made up of two compounds, *sym-ballein,* meaning to bring or throw together. People, however, use the words 'symbol/symbolism' in various ways, so that we need to attend to the specific meaning intended. In general a symbol is a thing, word, action, image or word that points to a further meaning beyond itself. The simplest symbols are often called 'signs'. These have usually only one meaning, such as traffic indications about speeds, hospitals, schools, features of the road; they primarily convey information. Scientific signs such as π, $+$, ∞, or $♀♂$ which indicate respectively the ratio of a circumference of a circle to its diameter (3.14159...), addition, infinity and female/male in genetics, all have their own one clear sense. Such signs are usually called 'arbitrary' in that there is no intrinsic connection between the sign and its meaning; they are also called 'conventional' because there is agreement about their significance in a place or even internationally: red indicates danger, an image of a plane shows the direction of an airport.

Symbol in a stricter sense is an image that is affective: it evokes a feeling or is evoked by a feeling. A clenched fist, a national flag or anthem, a Christmas card, all do more than convey information. They touch our imagination and involve the area of feeling. Circumstances will determine the depth of feeling: a Tricolour or Union Flag may have little effect on us when seen abroad flying with other EC flags; either could be quite provocative or welcoming in a particular street or village in the North of Ireland. Again saluting flags and the rules for respecting them, e.g. national flags are not to be flown after sunset, nor to be allowed to touch the ground, all point to affective values much greater than belongs to a piece of coloured cloth.

True symbols are said to be polysemantic, that is, they can have several meanings. A material thing may have an independent existence, for instance a rose growing in a garden. But a single rose laid on, or dropped into, a grave can be filled with profound meaning. Those observing this action may interpret it differently. The same reality may have widely different denotations. Water is such a symbol, pointing to very contrasting ideas: a glass of water to cooling and refreshing; a pump or oasis in a desert to life and fertility; a basin or bath to cleansing; a flood or angry sea to destruction; a stream, lake or waterfall to relaxation; a dam to power, etc. Pilate washed his hands to indicate that he was not guilty of Jesus' death. Again, people will be variously moved by the same symbol, even when they share the same meaning, e.g. a family meal or wedding celebration will be differently appreciated by the participants.

Dreams are very important symbols, which enable us to deal in a healthy way with our unconscious or suppressed memories. They usually have many layers of meaning. The meaning of some dreams is obvious; the interpretation of other dreams may need skilled help.

Symbols moreover at times may be the main, or indeed the only expression of some deep experiences. A symbol is often a non-verbal communication. Holding or hugging a person in distress is a very powerful way of support, empathy, sympathy or compassion (the last two both meaning 'suffer with'). Again, people such as monarchs, presidents, pop stars, religious or inspirational figures, or people in distress can focus our thoughts and draw our feelings in a specific direction: we may wish to emulate the person, follow their lead or guidance, take up some project under their inspiration; on the other hand burning their effigy would be a sign of contempt or rejection. Such symbolic persons also communicate more powerfully than any detached essay, no matter how profound. Again, poetry, the visual arts and music communicate in a way that rational or conceptual discourse cannot achieve. Symbols are particularly important in literature, especially in poetry. Here they provide an entry into a whole area of affectivity that is not easily touched by prose.

Symbols can operate for good or evil. The Nazi swastika, pornography, and racist emblems are destructive symbols. A positive symbol is the Red Cross (Red Crescent in Muslim countries), which rallies people to care for sick and wounded in war or in catastrophes and to uphold proper treatment of prisoners in times of conflict. The American Statue of Liberty was a positive symbol of a nation that welcomed people and gave them a new beginning. The shamrock and the harp are positive reminders of Irish identity, whereas shillelaghs and leprechauns can be symbols of stage-Irishism and hence rather negative. The Cross sums up the central mystery of Christian love.

Some symbols belong mainly to a particular place, e.g. the shamrock to Ireland. Others have a more complex life depending on various places, e.g. a harp is a symbol of Ireland, of an airline, of a brewer, of St Cecilia the patroness of music, of heaven (as in the phrase 'gone to play the harp'), of tediousness or boredom (as in phrase 'to harp on' from the monotony of an ill-played harp), etc.

Language

Language is symbolic. Words indicate a reality. The phonetic sound *ōk* indicates in English a genus of tree *(Quercus)* of the beech family; in Irish and Italian the words, *dair* and *quercia* respectively indicate the same tree. Language is conventional: we cannot decide to avoid the word 'oak' and make up our own word *ari* instead; we simply would not be understood, if we spoke about the *ari* in the field. We may have to explain what an oak is like to a person who has never seen one. We are constantly learning new words that can be particular to some science or activity: sport, music popular and classical, sciences, technology and even relatively simple activities like cooking (e.g. baste, braise, marinade) have their own terms that must be learned by asking or by observing how they are used. Moreover, people can create new words, or neologisms, which in time become current and to an extent unchangeable. Such new words are most often technical within a trade, science, area of study, group or culture. Ordinary words may change meaning; most teachers will have the experience of using what they thought was an ordinary word, but which provoked sniggers from the class. Text-messaging has its own language which seems to become progressively more obscure, at least to an older generation.

Modern linguistics has many theories of language and of the role of symbolism. Without getting too involved in these questions we can usefully explore some characteristics of language. Language is usually words, but not any words. The words must have meaning. Thus this following would seem correct in grammar, but has no meaning: 'Carrots love purple parachutes.' Moreover, language reveals something of the speaker. I may get only a very limited idea of persons from a photograph. When I hear them speak they already reveal something about themselves. Moreover, I normally speak to someone; speaking to oneself or a tree is not very common behaviour. But when I speak, I am inviting or looking for a response; I will not persevere in speaking to a person who is asleep or otherwise totally inattentive. The response I seek may merely be other person's interest. I may, however seek information ('what is the time, please?'), or wish that he or she did something. Speaking backed up by action is especially powerful.

Universal symbols

Some symbols are universal and are called transcultural, for instance the heart is a symbol of love, passion, and commitment to a person or cause. Psychologists coming after Sigmund Freud (d. 1939) and Carl Jung (d. 1961) speak of archetypical symbols, which arise from the deep subconscious or are seen as otherwise implanted in, or arising from, human nature itself. These universal symbols have been classified in very many ways, e.g. related to the four primitive elements of earth, water, air and fire; or related to primitive geometrical shapes: circle, square, centre, cross. The French anthropologist Gilbert Durand writing in the 1960s gave a useful classification of archetypical symbols and symbolic activity that is widely accepted. They are based on the development of children to adulthood as they take possession of their space. Firstly, to the activity of standing erect are clustered such symbols of ascent, the head, heavens and consequently of sun and light, separation and hence of purification. Secondly, to the activity of nourishment can be gathered symbols of descent, the mother, intimacy, womb, house, places of refuge and caring. Thirdly, to the activity of walking correspond symbols of life, departures, progress, means of transport, roads and rivers. Finally, there is the circle, which draws in sexual symbolism, cycles of life and death, new life, the wheel, the lunar and solar cycles.

There is, furthermore, a series of symbols based on interpersonal relationships. Some of these are seen as ascending: symbols of fatherhood to which corresponds the religion of the heavenly God. Others are viewed as descending: the symbol of the mother, which in various cultures can stress fecundity or destruction. The symbol of spouse is not primarily about fertility, but rather of friendship and love. The symbol of the hero brings in the drama of the human condition, the struggle against death. Freudian interpretations of symbols stress their relation to the past history of an individual, and are frequently negative; Jungian interpretations tend to emphasise the thrust towards the future and towards transformation of archetypical symbols.

Symbols in religion

Symbols arise from people's contact with their environment, with their history. Symbolic language has the characteristic of moving from the image to another level. All religions use symbols as well as ritual, which is often an extended or activated symbol. These are a means by which humans who are both corporeal and spiritual can communicate about and with the deity that is purely spiritual.

Some symbols, the archetypical ones, arise from our human nature and are found in almost all cultures. We find them particularly in folklore and in religion. They are the means whereby we communicate, especially about cultural experience. Religious experience moreover can only be communicated through symbol. Furthermore, religion is very much concerned not so much with God as a Being wholly other than us, but as an infinite, spiritual being with whom humans, men and women, can relate. Ascent symbols are particularly common in religion. Thus the religious symbolism of a mountain can be moral or spiritual exertion, but so too are a ladder and a tower in mystical writing; mountains, as the points of the world closest to the sky, can also be symbols of divine meeting.

The Judaeo-Christian Tradition

The Old Testament in all its books, historical, prophetic and wisdom, is replete with symbols of all kinds. The religious experience of the Hebrew people and later Christians centred on a God who created, cared for and saved his people. Some powerful symbols of this core religious experience were that of God as Father (e.g. Isa 9:6; Hos 11:1-4; Ps 89:26) and less frequently Mother (see Is 66:13), King (e.g. Ps 95:3), Shepherd (Ps 23), Vinedresser (Is 5:1-7), Deliverer and Saviour (Isa 49:26), Jealous Spouse (Hos ch. 2). God's power is also conveyed by symbols such as a Lion (Am 1:2; 3:8). The relationship between God and his people was frequently described with legal symbols like covenant, which was a particular form of contract, with warm interpersonal symbols of family, espousals, marriage and friendship. There were, too, symbols of alienation and sin: people were said to go astray, to disobey, to rebel, to offend God, to be unfaithful or commit adultery, to incur debt or guilt. Sin digs an abyss or erects a barrier between sinners and God (Isa 59:2 – the whole chapter has many symbols of sin). External ritual purity is a symbol of inner righteousness. Above all the sojourn in Egypt is seen as an image of sin and slavery, and the Exodus is a paradigm for all freedom and deliverance. God's plan for his people is expressed symbolically as the new or heavenly Jerusalem (see the abundance of symbols in Isa ch. 54 and Rev ch. 21), as a marriage, as a well-tended vineyard, and as the sacred Passover Meal.

In the New Testament the word 'symbol' does not occur. The equivalent is, however, 'mystery,' which has the sense of something hidden but now (partly) revealed, such as God's plan for salvation in Christ (Rom 16:25-16; Eph 3:1-10). In the gospel of John we have the word 'sign' which is an action revealing the meaning of Jesus and his message (John 2:11; 4:54). The notion of sacrament shares this duality of something visible and something invisible.

In the New Testament we encounter innumerable symbols, most notably the powerful symbol of Kingdom in the life and ministry of Jesus. He also presented himself under various symbols: 'I am bread of life ... the bread that has come down from heaven' (Jn 6:34.41); 'I am the light of the world' (Jn 8:12); 'I am the way, and the truth, and the life' (Jn 14:6). The Pauline writings present Jesus as the first-born of humanity (Rom 8:29; Col 1:15.18), as the head of all things (Eph 1:22) and head of the Body the Church (Col 1:18; Eph 5:23). The followers of Jesus are urged to be salt of the earth and light for the world (Matt 5:13.14). Through baptism they are symbolically buried and raised with Christ (Rom 6:3-4). Indeed all the sacraments are symbols, using primitive materials such as oil, water, bread, wine, and primitive gestures of blessing and touching.

Historical events can attain the status of symbol. Abraham's departure from Haran (Gen 12:1-6) becomes a symbol of other divine calls; and the Exodus of the people from Egypt (Exod ch. 12) a symbol of liberation. Again, biblical figures can be symbolic of exceptional qualities: 'A Daniel come to judgement' (Merchant of Venice; see Dan ch. 13), or 'wise as Solomon' (see 1 Kgs 3:5-15). Other people would use the word 'analogy' in these last two cases, indicating a partial resemblance

In religion there can be a rich symbolism of numbers: three and seven are often seen as perfect numbers; forty indicates completion or an indefinitely long period as in forty years of wilderness exile, forty days of the Lord's fast. Again, the Jewish menorah, a candlestick usually with seven branches, signifies true worship.

All these Judaic and Christian symbols share the characteristics we noted above: each symbol has a rich variety of meaning; each one can be grasped at different levels by various people. These symbols make possible a grasp of religious truth, which is attainable only through symbols. They are intellectual, appealing to reason; volitional, appealing to desire; and affective, appealing to feelings.

Later developments

The first 1,500 years of the Christian era was profoundly marked by symbols in all areas of life, religious and secular. In Ireland there was a strong sense of deep symbols. We have only to look at Newgrange to see remains of a culture whose symbolic language was extraordinarily powerful, but not fully clear to us. Many of the pre-Christian symbols were transformed. Wells with a pagan significance were given a Christian meaning, often being linked with a saint and healing.[1] Indeed, symbols were at times so extravagant that core values could be obscured. After the Reformation various currents of thought opposed symbols. The radical reformers rejected many of the religious symbols of the Catholic Church. Some like Oliver Cromwell (d. 1658) were called 'Puritans' because they sought a pure religion freed from ritual, ornaments and symbols as well as what they saw as other non-scriptural excrescences. In general, one can say that Reformation Christianity emphasised preaching and the word over ritual and symbolism. In the secular world about the same time the new sciences arose which distrusted the lack of precision of symbols. In the late seventeenth and throughout the eighteenth century, some religious thinkers, called Deists, modelled themselves on science and sought a natural religion, which was devoid of revelation and mystery. In the nineteenth century, with the Romantic Movement in poetry and the arts symbols made a comeback. At the turn of the twentieth century, especially in the Catholic Church, there was what was judged to be an excessive use of symbols in the so-called Modernist Movement. Its critics, especially Pope St Pius X (d. 1914), saw one of the dangers of Modernism to be a tendency to reduce faith to religious experience and symbols, whilst denying or neglecting the reality to which faith and symbols point. After the condemnations of Modernism for a variety of reasons, Catholic theology avoided any emphasis on symbols or subjective experience and concentrated on the objective content of revelation. It was only around the time of the Second Vatican Council (1962-1965) that theologians again spoke with confidence about symbols, particularly when dealing with sacraments.

A wider use of sacrament itself arose. Traditionally sacrament was an exterior symbol, which pointed to inner grace: water and specific words in baptism pointed to new life in God and membership of the Christian community. The word 'sacrament' became applied to Christ, who points to the Father and the life of the Trinity. The Church was then called a sacrament, pointing to Christ.

Other religions
Other religions also have rich symbolism, which makes religious discourse possible. In what are called 'primitive religions', that is, religions without a book, we can have highly sophisticated symbols based on places (mountains, rivers, sea), objects (trees, food, animals, garments), gestures, actions and movement (bodily marks and mutilations, rituals). Many of these religions also use symbols in common with the Judaic-Christian religions: the sky as the abode of God, sacrifices, and meals. And they are familiar with the archetypical symbols of light and darkness, life and death, guilt and burdens.

Some of these symbols feature in the great world religions. Thus Islam is constructed on five pillars. It knows ninety-nine names of God, most of them highly symbolic. There are holy places such as Mecca. There is a sacred garment called the *ihram* worn on arriving at Mecca. Ritual washings symbolise the inner purity needed to approach the holy place.

In Buddhism and Hinduism there are many sacred places, sacred rivers to allow access to the absolute or to God. Symbols common to Christian are also found, e.g. heart, tree, journey, light/darkness, or purifications.

The birth and death of symbols

Some symbols are deliberately created by a person or group. In time they may gain acceptance and be found fruitful or valuable. Many symbols die or no longer speak to many people, e.g. the rich symbolism of Greek and Latin mythology, the medieval symbols of dragons, unicorns, fairy princes and princesses. The Harry Potter and the Lord of the Rings books and films contain powerful symbols of the struggle between good and evil. Whether their symbols will become widely received in our culture remains to be seen.

A particular area of concern for Christian religious symbolism is that much of it arose from rural pastoral or agricultural communities in which tribal values still obtained. Thus symbols of vines, of shepherds, of agrarian men and women and their works of sowing, harvesting, of tribal marriage customs, of lakeside commercial fishing, and so forth may not mean much to urban dwellers. The fact that this symbolism is found in normative books of revelation presents a special problem.

With the philosopher Eric Voeglin we can consider four stages in the life of a symbol. The first stage is the engendering experience of the symbol. The baptismal symbolism arose from the preaching and practice of John the Baptist (see Luke 3:1-22), from the teaching and command of Jesus (see Matt 28:18-20; John 3:3-8; Mk 16:16) and from the practice and experience of the early Church (see Acts 2:38-41; 8:11-16; 19:1-7). The second stage in the life of a symbol is a period of reflection. This commenced already in New Testament times (e.g. Rom 6:1-11; Tit 3:4-7). This reflection has continued ever since in the preaching of the Church and in its liturgies. A third stage can come about when people lose contact with the engendering experience. People can seek baptism without very great sense of its meaning. Then we can have either fideism when people hold on to the symbol, repeating what has always been said, or else belief in the symbol that is at variance with its meaning. Thus people can seek baptism for their children for social reasons, to obtain entry into a particular school, or they may see it as bringing luck or protection. At this stage the symbol is under serious threat. A secular instance of loss of meaning might be the Irish flag. Its colours are often described as green-white-yellow, or green-white-gold, but it is more correctly green-white-orange. In the nineteenth century there were attempts to unite two cultures: one was Irish and Catholic symbolised by green; the other Protestant and Scottish symbolised by the English king William of Orange. If one says that the Irish flag is yellow or gold, one has lost contact with the engendering experience, which was an attempt to bring together the two cultures indicated by green and orange. So far have people lost contact with the symbolism that even its name is differently pronounced: trîcolour (with long *i* for Catholics) and tricolour (with short *i* for Protestants).

The fourth stage is a meditative reconstruction, in which we look again at the engendering experience. In the case of the Irish flag we might look at Irish history since the 1690s. If we feel passionately for national harmony and reconciliation, then the flag may take on again its symbolic meaning. The Church is always concerned that people return to the full meaning of baptism. Hence we have renewal of baptismal promises occasionally at Mass, and we have the Easter Vigil, which symbolically reenacts salvation history.

If the meditative reconstruction does not come about, the symbol may persist in a weak form in the third stage; it will no longer be a bearer of meaning or affectively touch people. It will eventually die or lose all relevance. There are many areas, not only in religious education, where teachers can walk with young people in the rediscovery of symbols. The power of symbols lies in the fact that they appeal not only to cold reason but also at the level of feeling.

Notes
1. E. Healy, *In Search of Ireland's Holy Wells* (Dublin: Wolfhound, 2001).

Select Bibliography
P. Béruerie and C. Duchesneau, *How to Understand the Sacraments* (London: SCM, 1991).

S. Happel, 'Symbol' in *The New Dictionary of Sacramental Worship*, ed. P.E. Fink. (Dublin: Gill and Macmillan/Collegeville: Liturgical Press, 1990) pp. 1237-1245.

K. Richter, *The Meaning of the Sacramental Symbols: Answers to Today's Questions* (Collegeville: Liturgical Press) 1990.

2

Ritual

Like the concept of symbol that we have considered in the last chapter, the related notion of ritual cannot be defined in a universally acceptable way. Both rite and ritual are considered by a huge variety of experts: anthropologists, psychologists, sociologists, and historians of religions, liturgists and theologians, to name but some of the specialists that study them. Again, these scholars come from many backgrounds; there are, for example, studies of ritual from Freudian, Jungian, Marxist perspectives, as well as from the standpoint of various Christian denominations, such as Catholic, Protestant and Orthodox. As in the previous chapter, we begin with some indications about the all-pervasiveness of ritual before focusing on its importance in religious, particularly Christian contexts.

Secular ritual

It is said that the modern age is allergic to ritual; technology and scientific rationality have little time for ritual, which of itself might not seem practical or immediately useful. But, on the contrary, we are all familiar with many rituals in our own lives. For example, we probably do more or less the same things and in the same order when we dress each morning. This ritual allows us to get through a process relatively painlessly and without much thought: we don't have to make a big decision in deciding whether or not to attend to our hair before we put on our shoes. We have a pattern. If we were asked why we do one thing before another in the mornings, we might or might not be able to give a reason. Again, we go to a supermarket, grab a trolley or basket, walk around the shop perhaps even in a particular direction, and end up at the cash desk. Such rituals, and there are many of them in our lives, are helpful, even though we can and do vary them at will.

There are also social rituals found in the way we greet one another: one way for a close friend, other ways for casual acquaintances, for people we have not seen for some time, for strangers, for people of our own age and milieu, for those different from us. There are also various rituals found at school, at a doctor's or dentist's surgery, and so forth. There are acceptable ways of behaving, rituals in every circumstance of our lives.

Some of these rituals are quite informal. Others that govern games can be quite elaborate: breaking some of them will be seen as discourteous or unacceptable; breaking others can lead to penalties according to the rules of the game. There are more public rituals found for example in Dáil Éireann, in the installation of mayors with chain of office, in courts of justice, in school, in the army, in Church.

Of particular importance are the rituals that are associated with what the French anthropologist, Arnold van Gennep, first called 'the rites of passage'. These mark new stages or transitions in life: birth, puberty, marriage and death; initiation rites are also found in various situations. In secular society birth, marriage and death bring people together; there is usually a meal and in Ireland drinking together. An equivalent of puberty rites are found in Jewish circles, called Bar Mitzvah, though strictly speaking the focus is on taking up religious responsibilities at about the age of thirteen.

So we can see ritual in our own private lives, in our environment, in our society and state. These are generally good and enable reasonable people to live and interact together. Ritual gives security and ease in our various activities and in the diverse situations in which we find ourselves. But we must be in control of such rituals; they are not to dominate our lives. For there are also unhealthy rituals in some people's lives that are called obsessive: people feel that they *have to do* certain things and in a certain order, otherwise they may feel guilty, distressed or feel that some misfortune may come upon them as a result of omitting some ritual. When extreme, such behavior can be a form of emotional or neurotic illness.

Ritual may be said to be conscious and voluntary, repetitious and symbolic bodily actions or words that seem appropriate to given situations. The key words are conscious – for ritual, unlike symbolism, does not take place in sleep. A second key idea is repetition, some once-off, or newly created series of actions or words would not yet be ritual. However, a stylised set of actions or words at some inauguration might be called ritual, but only because it is based on similar actions in other like situations. In the fullest sense of the word, ritual is also communal, that is, performed with others. Ritual has the possibility of unifying a group for a particular occasion. We can think of cutting a cake at a wedding, ordination meal or anniversary: everybody wants to see the action and are joined with the celebration of the principal figures who actually cut the cake; photographs are taken; there will be a usual ritual gesture of approval and celebration by applause and perhaps a song.

In public and secular life there can be great importance attached to who performs a ritual act. A new bridge or road will be officially opened by a ribbon being cut. It will often be a politician who performs this act. There are complex reasons. Politicians, whose oxygen is publicity, are happy to be associated with the important local event. The people involved are pleased to have their new road or bridge opened by somebody significant. It gives some standing to the community. We would never dream of a person being selected for such a task by putting one thousand names of local residents into a hat, and picking one to do the ceremony. There may be lesser roles for others in a ritual, such as presenting flowers, driving a car or horse and cart over the new road, and so on. While such secular rituals have a clear meaning, not everybody will attach the same importance to them

Ritual in modern society

We have seen that ritual pervades all our lives. But the form that a ritual takes depends to a great extent on the identity or a group and on the bonds that they share. Large urban populations do not have elaborate rituals, but groups within the population may. Cults, for example, have strong bonding and very often an elaborate and oppressive ritual.

As we have noted, it is often stated that modern culture is anti-ritualistic. The truth is not so simple. We can note factors that are not favorable to ritual in our society. Firstly, the modern technological age stresses efficiency; ritual is not productive of an immediate tangible good. Secondly, our age stresses rationality and logic in activities; ritual belongs also to the area of affectivity. Thirdly, our world is one of rapid change and splintering; ritual is oriented towards values like order and stability. Fourthly, modern society stresses what is objective and verifiable; ritual is often apprehended subjectively and evaluated by individuals. Fifthly, contemporary society is marked by pluralism in society, arts and religion; ritual operates most easily where there is a shared world-view. Sixthly, our world is characterised by many ideologies, ethical positions and values; ritual flourishes where there are common values and assumptions.

But paradoxically ritual re-emerges in many ways. There is a reaction in society to the harsh rationalism of technology and science, and to the greed and aggressiveness of consumerism. Increasingly in popular magazines we have talk of other values: the right-side brain which is concerned with intuition rather than the rationality of the left-side; feminine values rather than patriarchal ones; spirituality of various kinds in place of materialism; New Age as an alternative both to traditional religion and to modern secularism. All of these recent orientations are once again open to ritual. Furthermore, the very societies that were most opposed to ritual – one thinks of the former Soviet block and Communist China – draw powerfully on ritual, especially rites of confession in show-trials as well as extended symbols of Communist achievement and military might. Even Churches that were rather cool towards ritual are rediscovering the power of ceremonial.

Taboo

An important feature of ritual, especially religious ritual, is the complex notion of taboo. Originally the words referred to what was holy or unclean. It came to mean what is felt to be prohibited, unthinkable and could lead to ostracism. Thus pork or other swine meat for many Jews and Moslems is forbidden. The origins may have been hygienic; pork is notoriously a dangerous food in hot climates unless well refrigerated – even in Ireland it was formerly avoided in those summer months that did not have an 'R'. But for the Jew and the Moslem such meat is felt to be revolting because in some sense it is now felt to be unclean.

Earlier scholars thought of taboo as arising from fear or suppressed longing. Its function would appear rather to be social, and it involves keeping order. Thus sexual taboos ensure reverence for others and ourselves, and help to secure becoming behavior. They protect roles in the family, in institutions and in the wider society. There is a powerful taboo against incest. Physical attacks on certain persons, e.g. parents, religious leaders, members of the Garda Síochána, are regarded as particularly reprehensible by society. Religious taboos remind us of the sacred. Sacrilege is a taboo which ensures that sacred things and places must be properly respected. Desecration of a place of worship, of a cemetery or of an important national memorial are felt to be particularly repugnant. What is seen as holy or otherwise sacred is protected by taboos.

Religious ritual

Religious ritual is found in connection with the sacred, often called the 'numinous' (from Latin *numen,* divinity). In general, the sacred has a mysterious reality that is wholly different from ordinary or 'natural' realities. But though different, the sacred and the ordinary are not separated; people seek from the sacred both meaning and underpinning for their lives. Religious ritual emphasises the difference of the divine world from the ordinary world. Hence we can find different clothes, altered manner of speech, special places and times.

Religious ritual gets its meaning from what is called 'myth' by anthropologists and students of religion. 'Myth' here is a technical term and does not mean what is false or a fable without foundation. It means the story of origins, what gives meaning to a society or group. The Battle of the Boyne in 1690 is a myth in this sense; it certainly happened in history. But as recalled in the Unionist community, it gives an understanding of its origins and a vindication of its present. In Christianity the key myth is the life, death and resurrection of Jesus. These certainly happened at the beginning of our era. They are celebrated in ritual and give the origins and meaning of the Christian religion. There are other religious myths, which unlike the Christian one are not historical, e.g. the stories of the Greek and Roman gods, the Hindu gods. These are not properly speaking false, for they do enlighten the adherents of the religion about the meaning of human existence, and even partially about the divine mystery.

Religious ritual seeks to put us in contact with a significant past. Some African and Aboriginal Australian religions wish to put the participants in touch with the origins of the world and its creation by the god(s). Christian ritual seeks to put us in living contact with the death and resurrection of Jesus.

Elements of religious ritual
In the ritual of what are called the 'higher religions' there is an important place for the sacred written text or scriptures. Other religions do not have a book, but they can have very profound oral traditions. These religions used to be lumped together and called 'animist' or 'primitive'. They are now more properly called 'traditional'.

Another feature of religious ritual is chant and music, occasionally extemporised, but more usually determined from earlier occasions. Likewise prayers and intercessions can be stylised or spontaneously created by the worshipper.

Food and drink are given a sacral meaning in religious ritual. These may be used in sacrifice, which means that they are transferred to the divine sphere and are at the same time a means of contact with the divine; that is to say, they are mediatorial. In the Old Testament there was an elaborate ritual of worship (see Exod chs. 25-31).

A particularly important section of Old Testament ritual is what is called 'The Law of Holiness' (Lev chs. 17-26). This probably dates towards the end of the monarchy (sixth century BCE) and relates to the time of temple. Holiness is one of the essential attributes of God (see Lev 11:44-45). The original concept of holiness is one of separateness, of inaccessibility and of awe-inspiring transcendence (see Exod 33:18-20). This sanctity communicates itself to everything consecrated to God: places (see Exod 19:12), seasons (see Lev 23:1-8), the ark (see 2 Sam 6:7-8), people (see Exod 19:3) and priests in particular (see Lev 21:6), as well as things (see Exod 30:25-29). Because holiness was thought of in relation to worship, it is connected with the idea of ritual purity: the 'law of holiness' is also a 'law of purity'. But the God of Israel also made moral demands and so the primitive notion of holiness was transformed: attention moved from what was ritually impure to abstention from sin and so ritual purity develops into purity of conscience.[1]

Some Hebrew sacrifices involved eating part of what was sacrificed, some belonged to the priest (see Num 18:8-10), and the rest was burned and seen as belonging to God (Lev 3:1-17; 7:11-38). In this meal people were united with God. In some cultures sacrifices are mainly of animals and the blood is seen as significant. In other religious, such as Hinduism, flowers are a preferred sacrifice. They may afterwards be shared among the worshippers. After the fall of the Third Temple in 70 CE Jewish rabbis taught that prayer, almsgiving and works of charity could replace the former sacrifice of animals and crops. Protestant Christians in practice take up a somewhat similar position.

Since there is a human sense that our actions or we can be flawed, religious ritual often has a role for the admission of guilt and failure, in order to be re-centered or healed.

Sacred time reflects cosmic time, the seasons or the cycles of human life. Time is seen to wax and wane like organisms, it is marked by growth and decay and must be regenerated. In secular society we have New Year rituals, which has a sense of new beginning. In religions we have sacred times, the month of Ramadan in Islam, the Passover and other feasts of Judaism, the Christian feasts and the Liturgical Year.

Different types of ritual
Some anthropologists speak of two broad kinds of religious ritual. The first is *confirmatory*. This seeks to preserve order between people and the divine. Examples are religious greetings, blessings, and prayers that help people to discover and maintain awareness of the divine presence in the world, e.g. prayers before meals. Taboos belong to confirmatory

ritual. The second kind is called *transformatory* ritual, which seeks to change people in relation to the divine, or a sacred. These include rituals of consecration, for example, ordination of people, religious vows, and initiation rites, blessing a house or place. This second category also includes conversion rituals, which bring people from guilt or sin to some new life. Other scholars subdivide further the second category so that there are rituals of *restoration* which seek healing, purification and also what are called *crisis rites,* for example, invocation and intercessions at a time of sickness, natural disasters or societal evils.

Ritual as personal and collective

We have seen that there can be personal rituals in a person's life. These can be secular or religious. Some attention will be given to the latter in the next part on prayer. Religious ritual generally, however, is thought of as societal or collective. Ritual often expresses group identity, the memory of a people as seen in its traditions, the meaning of its communal existence. Moreover, it often seeks to make present the sacred past of a people. Individuals who take part in collective ritual are challenged to become involved in what is being done. This participation may be purely internal; they agree with what is being celebrated. There may also be external approbation by word or deed, e.g. by chant, words, dance, movement, and offering. Vatican II described the ideal for Catholic worship as 'full, active and conscious' participation (Vatican II, *Liturgy,* SC 14).

Ritual celebration is less than ideal when there is any breakdown or lack of coherence between the external ritual and the inner dispositions of the worshipper. The extent of commitment of an individual varies enormously even in the same individual during the same ritual at different times, e.g. a Catholic at Mass, a Moslem performing the daily prayers.

Ritual can have a double function: it may be educative, communicating truths or teaching to those involved (Vatican II, *Liturgy*, SC 33-36); these functions may have the value of social cohesion for a group and they may also benefit the individual.

Ritualism

Ritualism has various meanings. It often means attaching significance to ritual; it can also have the overtone of excessive or undue importance. There are several issues involved here. Ritual is notoriously conservative and change can often be disturbing. We have only to look at the Catholic Church after Vatican II when enormous change in liturgy was very unevenly received, or at the varied torturous attempts at change of *The Book of Common Prayer* in the Anglican Communion, reflected in the Church of Ireland's various Service Books. A similar parallel is the profound attachment of so many members of the Church of England to the magnificent, if archaic, prose of the King James Bible.

Ritual adaptation: the Roman Catholic experience

The experience of these two Christian bodies, the Roman Catholic Church and the Anglican Communion, shows us something of the difficulties involved with any changes of ritual. We might illustrate it in considering the liturgy of the Eucharist, in various traditions called the Mass, the Lord's Supper, Holy Communion and the Breaking of Bread. In the early centuries the ritual was informal and celebrated in the language of the people. Early in the second century there is an attempt to formalise the celebration.[2] Other attempts soon followed, especially from the fourth century; from the time of the first emperor of the Holy Roman Empire, Charlemagne (d. 812), there was much unification of liturgy. By the high Middle Ages the celebration had become increasingly remote from ordinary people. The language had been frozen in an austerely beautiful Latin. There were two forms of celebration: a High

Mass with several ministers, music, elaborate ceremonies and incense; and a Low Mass celebrated in barely audible tones by a single priest with a congregation which might consist only of one server. At the time of the Reformation there was a reform of the liturgy and a simplification of many ceremonies that had been added over the years. This reform gave what is sometimes called the Tridentine Mass promulgated by Pope St Pius V in 1570. The next major reform was after Vatican II when there was further simplification, a return to the vernacular languages, and great emphasis on participation by all present.

Some in the Church have vigorously opposed these changes, even to the point of disobedience and movement into schism. For others the changes did not go far enough, so at times in disobedience they moved to various alternative or radically modified liturgies. The main problem with what is here called disobedience is the fact that liturgy and especially the Eucharist are a communal celebration of the Church and its ritual cannot be left to individual decisions or whim. Liturgical ritual belongs to the community, which needs to be protected from arbitrary and/or ill-informed novelties imposed by priest or minister. On the other hand, there is some leeway in liturgical books for adaptations for various situations and needs.

In the Catholic Church there are further problems emerging from the four decades of liturgical reform that have followed since Vatican II. Liturgists will rightly point to a failure on the part of priests and congregations to embrace ritual reforms in worship. But there is a deeper problem. In some way we can say that ritual has become impoverished since the Council. Older people will remember processions and varied liturgies like Benediction. In such rituals people had a more active role, compared with the present liturgy is which movement is restricted to standing, sitting, kneeling, moving to the altar for Communion and taking part through responses and song. Older people regret the loss of a sense of mystery that helped them to worship. Atmosphere was created by the Latin language, as well as by incense, abundance of candles, genuflections, varied vestments and elaborate gestures by the priest. We would need to recognise that there is some loss with the liturgical reform. People need to have a more physical involvement. Hence the custom continues of lighting candles at shrines. This practice has more recently returned to Anglican cathedrals in England, where many light a candle at some sacred memorial. The meaning of such a candle can often be obscure. Some people just want 'to do something'. Others see the candle left behind as continuing their worship when they depart from the Church. People see candles as a sign of life, of reverence or of celebration.

Anglican experiences

The liturgical experience of the Anglican Communion has complex causes. In passing, we might note that the word 'Anglicanism' is nineteenth century; before that one spoke of the Church of England, Church of Ireland, etc. In considering its liturgy and ritual a most important consideration is the nature of Anglicanism, which seeks to be both Catholic and Reformed. From its Catholic heritage comes an esteem for ritual; from its Reformed, especially Calvinistic, history comes a distrust and at times disdain for ritual. At various times either of these two tendencies has been in the ascendant, as for instance in the sixteenth-century revisions of *The Book of Common Prayer* (BCP), which had first appeared in 1549; the 1662 revision which has remained until today gave a greater Protestant emphasis to the BCP. Further attempts at revision in this century ran into several difficulties: one was the problem of producing a text acceptable to all streams of Church of England thought. There was also the additional problem of Parliament regulating the worship of the Established Church.[3]

The Church of Ireland used the English 1662 BCP. When it became disestablished, that is no longer being a state Church in Ireland (1869), it had no difficulty in producing its own revision of the BCP in 1878 and recently an Irish BCP at the will of the Church manifested in Synod.[4] The Anglican Communion has had continual tensions in ritual between its Protestant and Catholic wings; these are often referred to respectively as Low Church and High Church. The Protestant heritage would favour worship that is centered on the word, proclaimed from the Bible and commented in a substantial sermon. The remainder of the service would consist of hymns and prayers. Congregations of the Protestant leaning would not have Holy Communion as the main Sunday service; in more recent times it is more frequent than the hitherto monthly celebration; then it will be at an earlier hour on Sunday. At services the presiding minister often is not elaborately dressed; Eucharistic vestments like chasuble are not used in this tradition. Instead an ankle-length black vestment, called a cassock or gown, is common – over which a shorter white linen surplice might be worn, as well as a black scarf, stole or university hood. Incense, candles and ornamentation are generally avoided in this Low Church Anglican tradition. The more Catholic wing, or 'High Church', approaches much more closely and often replicates Roman Catholic ritual, vestments, prayers, ornaments such as candles, and ceremonial such as incense. Holy Communion, often called Eucharist, is central in the ritual life of the congregation, often being celebrated daily.[5] We should note that features that have disappeared in the Roman Catholic churches are still valued in the High Church tradition: reservation of the Sacrament, Stations of the Cross and, in places, Gregorian chant and Benediction. The High Church seeks to appeal to all five senses and welcomes ritual. But everywhere in the Church of Ireland there is a very strong antipathy to anything that would be seen as in bad taste in language or gesture.

Evaluation of religious ritual
From these two Churches we see something of the tensions that ritual can generate, its naturally conservative tendency, and

its centrality in the lives of Church members. But we can also appreciate its value. As people come together regularly to pray, they cannot be endlessly creative. When a ritual occurs only seldom, e.g. a class-Mass once a term, then it is possible and desirable to put in a lot of effort to have a celebration meaningful to the group and expressing its life and hopes. But it is not realistic or even psychologically possible to have such creativity and involvement on a weekly, much less a daily basis. The established ritual is then a support enabling the community to worship without stress and fatigue. Again, I may have many worries or concerns on a particular day so that I may not at all feel like worship or much participation. On such occasions the established ritual can carry me, so that I can be helped and strengthened by the ritual that does not impose too strenuous a burden on me.

But ritual can have inherent weaknesses. For just as an act of worship can carry me in difficult moments, so too I can become too detached from what is celebrated so that the ritual can become empty for me. Religious ritual is not mere spectacle, which is enjoyed passively. It demands that people be involved at every level of their being. The complaint often heard that 'the Mass is boring' may well be true at the level of spectacle, but as religious ritual it calls on those present to participate, which most fundamentally means that they relate what is being celebrated with the whole of their lives. As in many other spheres of life, what you get out of Mass largely depends on what you put in.

Another problem arises when ritual is not truly integrated into life. Thus, other areas of the syllabus deal with ways in which one is genuinely a religious person. When authenticity in life-style is missing, then participation in ritual is flawed. At worst it can be seen as Pharisaism, which arises when there is a split between the exterior works of religion and the internal dispositions. Jesus frequently castigated some of the Pharisees of his time for such behaviour (see Matt 23:36; Luke 11:37-54), though it might be argued that Pharisees in other places and other times did not all merit such condemnation. But this trap of mere externalism is a constant threat to true worship; moreover it can lead to our condemnation and judgment of others who are not so precise about external ritual (see Luke 18:9-14). In a later chapter we shall see a similar problem about vocal prayer: we need to mean what we say and to have our prayers and our lives integrated.

There is another side to the problem of integration: people can be so active, even in good works, that they do not feel the need of worship. Activism can lead to a life that is just as one-sided, as in the case of the person who fails to integrate into his or her commitment to worship the cares of those in need of love and care.

Vatican II presents an ideal when it says in several places that 'the Eucharist is the source and the summit of the Christian life' (Vatican II, *Church*, LG 11), but also warns that personal prayer is needed by individuals (Vatican II, *Liturgy*, SC 12), and that conversion is required for authentic Christian life (Vatican II, *Liturgy*, SC 9). Everything is to be brought to the Eucharist and offered as a sacrifice to God (see Rom 12:1-2); from the Eucharist comes healing, strength and grace for all activities. In this way the problems of ritualism are diminished.

Notes

1. See note on Leviticus 17:1 in standard edition of *The New Jerusalem Bible* (1985).
2. See encyclopedias and standard reference works on St Hippolytus of Rome who was associated with The *Apostolic Tradition*, a document of Church Order, dated early in the third century.
3. See M.J. Hackett, 'Prayer Books' in *The Study of Anglicanism* edited by S. Sykes and J. Booty (London: SPCK/Philadelphia: Fortress, 1988) pp. 121-133.
4. *The Book of Common Prayer according to the use of the Church of Ireland* (Dublin: Columba, 2004) [Irish BCP]

5. On the Eucharist in Anglicanism see William R. Crockett, 'Holy Communion', *Study of Anglicanism* pp. 272-285.

Select Bibliography

P. Béruerie and C. Duchesneau, *How to Understand the Sacraments* (London: SCM, 1991).

S. Sykes and J. Booty, eds. *The Study of Anglicanism* (London: SPCK/Philadelphia: Fortress Press, 1988) (The perspective is more Church of England and Episcopal Church of America. For Church of Ireland see next title.)

The Book of Common Prayer according to the use of the Church of Ireland (Dublin: Columba, 2004).

J.F. White, *Introduction to Christian Worship* (Nashville: Arbingdon Press, 3rd revised ed. 2000). Ecumenical.

G.S. Worgul, 'Ritual' in *The New Dictionary of Sacramental Worship*, ed. P.E. Fink (Dublin: Gill and Macmillan/Collegeville: Liturgical Press, 1990) pp. 1101-1106.

3

Sacrament

We are by now getting used to the fact that the words in this part of the syllabus, perhaps more than in any other area of religious studies, do not have an univocal meaning, but are used differently in various religious traditions and by particular authors. Similarly with the word 'sacrament'. For the religious context with which we are here concerned, a dictionary may not be very much help, though it might alert us to root meanings in Latin: *sacramentum* having the sense of a (public) pledge or oath from *sacrare* signifying 'to consecrate'.

The reality behind the word is more complex. Sacramentality is a religious concept, but by no means confined to Christianity. It involves symbols, which relate human experience to divine presence and some consequent transformation of people both individually and socially. Since the divine is totally other from humans, contact is effected through symbols. God comes to the worshipper through a symbol, and the worshipper is changed as a result of the divine encounter. This last word is important because the human person meets God in and through the symbol. In this meeting there is a self-revelation of the divine, seen usually as caring or to be appeased; there is an opening of the worshipper to the divine influence. This meeting should lead to a change in the person: it may be initiation into new life, a consecration to God's ways, an acceptance of the divine will, pardon or mercy. The change may remain at the level of knowledge, but it can lead to a profound transformation in values and worldview.

Initiation rites

A look at initiation rites will give some sense of sacramentality in the religions of the world. Initiation rites have features that are common to many religions. They often take place at puberty. Symbols of death and life, or sleep and wakefulness are common. Thus, in some cultures, those who are to be initiated are brought into darkness: they are led into a tunnel, into a dark grove or covered with skins; they may be immersed momentarily in water; they may be physically marked or mutilated in some way. At this time they may be given knowledge hitherto withheld from them, particularly the 'myth' or story of origins. It is common to be given a special or new name at the time. The various initiation rites in world religions all have the sense of bringing a person from an old way to new life or to maturity, so that a new phase begins.

In initiation rites we find symbolic actions and words which have a meaning and are perceived by those taking part as having some power: they transfer the person to a new sphere in which they have a new relationship with the deity and with society. For the Jewish people circumcision, first seen to have a religious significance with Abraham, was such a symbolic action; it became moreover a sign of the covenant relationship of God with Abraham and his descendents (see Gen 17:9-14). Catholic theologians in the past have referred to circumcision as a sacrament of the Old Law.

The great sacraments: Christ and the church

In the Christian tradition sacraments are religious rites variously described as a channel or sign of grace. Roman Catholics speak of seven sacraments, but one can speak of more. Even if our view of sacrament is a limited one, e.g. a visible sign that gives grace or effects a positive change in a person, then it is obvious that Christ is a sacrament. And so is the Church. Jesus Christ is the Son of God who became clothed in humanity and was born of the Virgin Mary. He is in the fullest sense both God and man. He went about doing good and preaching Good News, was put to death and rose again (see Acts 10:36-40). The Jews recalled the Passover Lamb, whose power to save was very limited (see Exodus 12:1-17). Jesus, the Lamb of God (see John 1:36), came to take away our sins. Our salvation operated through Calvary and Easter is called the Paschal Mystery.

Even during his lifetime, people were puzzled by who Jesus was (see Matt 16:13-16; John 10:24). Jesus was the Messiah, who revealed the Father: 'who ever has seen me has seen the Father... I am in the Father and the Father is in me' (John 14:9-10); 'the Father and I are one' (John 10:30). The man Jesus therefore points beyond himself to the full mystery of God, and to God's will to save humanity. He is the visibility of God's grace. Hence modern theology will speak of Christ as the great or foundational sacrament: he is a sign of divine life for us all. Christ is also the foundational sacrament in that he is the source of all the sacraments.

The Church is also a sacrament, but in a secondary sense. We see the Church as a beautiful, if flawed, institution. At its best the Church is pointing beyond itself to the presence of God's love and salvation in the world. It makes divine life present through the scriptures, through its teaching and its life. At times, sin and scandal prevent people seeing this beauty, but it is nonetheless part of the reality of the Church. There are always more holy people than villains in it, though the latter make more news. We can speak of the Church as a sacrament, for it points beyond itself and can lead people to God's life.

When we speak of Christ and the Church being sacraments, we are indicating also that salvation is part of the great mystery revealed in Christ (see Eph 1:9; 3:9; 5:32). Indeed the word *mystêrion* in Greek (whence we get the word 'mystery' and its translation *'sacramentum'*) indicates what is partly revealed and partly hidden. An older theology used to speak of sacrament as 'a visible sign of invisible grace'. The word can therefore be used supremely about Christ and the Church, but also in a looser way about realities that have a deeper meaning for the religious person. Thus we can speak of creation as a sacrament, for it reveals God's wisdom and beauty, and leads us to wonder and contemplation. Spiritual writers of the Christian East speak of creation being an open book to those who love God.

The sacramental economy
The *Catechism of the Catholic Church* treats in detail of the sacramental economy (nn. 1076-1209). The word 'economy' (Greek *oikonomia* indicating order of a household) means fundamentally a plan or management, a dispensation. The Christian economy is, then, the way God has ordered salvation for his people. Its principal meaning is the Paschal Mystery of the death and resurrection of Jesus along with the sending of the Holy Spirit at Pentecost. Its wider meaning is the liturgy through which we celebrate and enter into God's plan. Liturgy is the rite of the community in worshipping God and in receiving God's gifts. The *Catechism* notes: 'In the Church's liturgy the divine blessing is fully revealed and communicated' (n. 1082). The liturgy is ritual that is directed to the Father through Jesus Christ in the power of the Holy Spirit (nn. 1110-1111). It is a ritual of the Church community in which individuals join to receive the gifts God has planned to give us in Christ Jesus.

We have seen earlier various kinds of ritual, secular and religious. We have also noted the danger of ritualism. What makes liturgy live is the Holy Spirit. The *Catechism* spells out the role of the Holy Spirit:

> The mission of the Holy Spirit in the liturgy of the Church is to prepare the assembly to encounter Christ; to recall and manifest Christ to the faith of the assembly; to make the saving work of Christ present and active by his transforming power; and to make the gift of communion bear fruit in the Church. (n. 1112)

The communion here is the rich New Testament word *koinonia*, which means sharing; it is sometimes translated as 'fellowship'. We are in communion with and sharing in God's life; we share life and are joined to one another in love and faith. In this sense communion is the whole purpose of sacraments. It is the Holy Spirit that brings about such sharing. Thus we have the text of 2 Cor 13:13 which is a greeting in Catholic liturgy, but often used as a blessing formula in other Churches: 'The grace of our Lord Jesus Christ, the love of God and the fellowship of the Holy Spirit be with you.' Holy Communion is a particular sharing with Jesus when he comes to us in his Body and Blood as heavenly food.

In general then we can say that God's plan for us is most visible and most available in the liturgy, in the sacramental life that has been given to the Church.

The sacraments of the Church

Jesus Christ ascended to heaven, but left us both the memorial of his death and resurrection and the Holy Spirit who would lead the Church into truth. In time the Church recognised rites which came from the Lord, which in the Western Churches are called 'sacraments', and in the Churches of the East 'mysteries'. The Catholic Church discerned these celebrations from the Lord to be seven; other Christian Churches would not agree with this number.

We can say that the sacraments are 'of the Church' in a double sense (n. 1118). Firstly, they are 'by the Church' for these rites are performed by the Church in the power of the Holy Spirit. Secondly, they are sacraments 'for the Church' in that it is these rites above all else that make the Church, constitute its reality and build it up. The Church without sacraments would be an empty shell.

The seven sacraments recognised by the Catholic Church and the Churches of the East are baptism, confirmation (or chrismation), Eucharist, penance (or reconciliation), anointing of the sick, orders and matrimony. Of these baptism and Eucharist are the most important. In some Protestant Churches only these two are recognised as sacraments. They can be grouped in various ways. There are the 'sacraments of initiation', which bring us to life in the Church, namely baptism, confirmation and Eucharist; there are the 'healing sacraments' of reconciliation and anointing of the sick; and there are the sacraments of service and the life of the community, namely marriage and orders.

Celebration of sacraments

It is the Church that celebrates the sacraments. We can speak of sacraments as a meeting or an encounter between an individual, who receives the sacrament, with and in the Church. There are various persons in this meeting. Firstly there is Christ, working through his Holy Spirit. It is the minister of the sacrament who brings about the meeting and who represents Christ and the wider Church. There are different ministers for the various sacraments. In most of the sacraments it is a priest or deacon; for orders it is a bishop. In marriage it is the wedded couple who minister and make Christ present to one another. In an emergency baptism can be given by anybody. Ideally, there should be some others present to represent the wider Church community.

An important notion in sacramental theology is that of presence. Vatican II spoke of various ways in which Christ is present:

To accomplish so great a work Christ is always present in his church, especially in liturgical celebrations. He is present in the sacrifice of the Mass both in the person of his minister, 'the same now offering, through the ministry of priests, who formerly offered himself on the Cross', and most of all in the sacramental species. By his power he is present in the sacraments so that whenever anybody baptises it is really Christ himself who baptises. He is present in his word since it is he who speaks when the holy scriptures are read in church. Lastly he is present when the church prays and sings, for he has promised 'where two or three are gathered together in my name there am I in the midst of them' (Matt 18:20).[1]

Though Christ is present in these four ways, we may not be aware of him. We can visit a sick person in hospital who may be asleep and oblivious of our presence. In sacraments we must not be passive, but alert, entering into what Christ is doing and opening ourselves to receive this teaching and his grace.

The sacramental symbol

The celebration, or sacramental encounter, is a complex symbol made up of various parts. In every sacrament there is some concrete matter and action, e.g. pouring water in baptism, exchanging consent in marriage. There are also words which make clear what is going on: for example, the minister says, 'I absolve you from your sins.' We obtain the meaning of the sacraments from either the material or action together with the words. This is the core symbol. Making up the symbol also are the minister representing both Christ and the Church, the recipient, that is, the person who is receiving the sacrament, and other members of the Church.

In the sacramental symbol there are elements that are visible or perceptible: people in the encounter, the materials such as bread and wine, the words used. Invisible are Christ and the

Holy Spirit, as well as the grace or divine life which is given. The symbol is therefore visible, but pointing to divine Persons and a reality that are not visible. Sacraments can thus be said to address our total reality, for the human person is both flesh and spirit.

In recent liturgical reform in the Catholic Church there is great emphasis on scripture. Before coming to the core of the sacrament we have scripture readings which alert us to God's plan at his time, assure us of his love and grace, and invite our response in faith (see *Catechism* 1153-1155).

Symbolic gestures in worship

We have seen the importance of symbols for encounter with God. There are many ways in which we can have non-verbal worship. In the Old Testament as well as in the Christian tradition there is a significant role for bodily movements, actions and gestures in worship.[2] Some of these are also shared with other faiths. One can give a general sense for these, but a particular ritual may have other meanings and a worshipper may have a different intention.

Postures

There are different postures, that is, ways in which we hold our bodies for some notable time. When there is a community at worship, a common posture symbolises the unity of the people in a common action. *Standing* indicates respect, our human and religious dignity. The Second Eucharist Prayer says, 'We thank you for counting us worthy to stand in your presence and serve you'. *Kneeling* can indicate an attitude of supplication and adoration (see Peter in Luke 5:8; Jesus himself in Luke 22:41). It is found in quiet personal prayer. In present Catholic practice, there is some variance from place to place about when one kneels or stands. *Sitting* at the time of Jesus was the posture of one teaching (see Mark 5:1). At present it is the gesture for times of reflection, meditation and the reception of instruction. *Prostration* is a dramatic posture that indicates the person's

complete submission to God. It is found at ordination rites, at
religious profession and on the Good Friday liturgy. Modern
church pews are not conducive to prostration. This gesture also
has the ancient meaning of *epiclêsis*, that is, prayer for the Holy
Spirit.

Actions

In worship we find that people change the position of their
bodies, or of limbs. This can have various meanings. *Bowing* is
the action of inclining the head or torso and symbolises
reverence. Contemporary Roman Catholic liturgy prescribes a
bow at the name of Jesus, Mary and the saint of the day.[3]
Genuflection, that is, 'bending the knee' is a sign of adoration,
especially for the reserved Sacrament. The priest genuflects at
the Elevation of the Host and chalice at Mass. *Turning towards the
East* was common in baptismal liturgies. The East from which
the sun rises is seen as a symbol for Christ; churches were
commonly built facing East, and so worshippers faced in this
direction, rather than West where the sun disappears into
darkness. *Processions* are of many kinds. They involve a
movement of people. Entry processions underline the truth of
life being a journey/pilgrimage; they can also be a shift from a
profane place to a sacred one. We have festive processions,
funeral processions, and processions as a form of supplication of
intercession. Particular feasts have their own processions: Palm
Sunday, Candlemas Day (2 February), Good Friday, and at
Corpus Christi people venerate the Blessed Sacrament carried in
procession. Religious movement is also found in the common
Roman Catholic devotion of the Stations of the Cross during
which the worshipper retraces fourteen stages of the Passion of
Jesus.

Gestures

We can speak of liturgical gestures when some part of the body
symbolically expresses an interior attitude. *Raising of eyes and*

hands are classical gestures of prayer. The *orans* position of prayer, with hands raised to shoulder level or above, is used by the president of liturgical celebrations. It is also common in icons of Mary who intercedes for the Church. *Folding hands*, that is putting them together, is found in private prayer, and as people process to receive Communion. *Striking the breast* is not very common today. It has strong biblical roots (see the tax-collector in Luke 18:13). It is found in the confession of sins or sinfulness at Mass. *Kissing sacred objects* is a profound reverence and respect for objects, especially when they symbolise Christ, such as a crucifix. At the beginning of Mass the priest kisses the altar to indicate its holiness. In churches of the Christian East icons are venerated with a kiss, as are relics in both East and West. *The kiss or sign of peace* is also ancient with biblical roots (see Rom 16:16; 1 Cor 16:20; 1 Pet 5:14). Here a universal gesture of affection is a symbol for the love and peace that should exist among Christians. It is found during worship, and at times can include a religious greeting. The *Sign of the Cross* on the forehead, or on the body (forehead, breast and two shoulders), is very ancient. It invokes the primary Christian symbol of our Redemption and identity in Christ. It is used also in sacraments to indicate the power of Christ who is the main minister of each sacrament. It is also a sign of blessing, as the love and grace of Christ is invoked over persons and things either in intercession or in a gesture that constitutes them as holy. In several sacraments we have a powerful symbol of *imposition of the hand(s)*. Touching in all cultures has various symbolic meanings. In the Old Testament we find imposition of hands as a gesture of power, as when Moses at God's command stretched out his hands over the sea and the waters were divided (see Exod 14:16.21). In sacramental use it has several meanings: a symbol of power or grace coming upon the recipient (see 1 Tim 4:14), a symbol of healing or reconciliation (frequent in the ministry of Jesus, e.g. see Mark 6:2.5; 16:18; Luke 13:13); a blessing (Matt 19:15); an invocation of the Holy

Spirit as in the Eucharist *epiclêsis* over the elements to be consecrated.

Finally, it is to be noted that in Masses for children gestures are recommended.[4]

Ritual development

In the early Church there were many ways of celebrating the sacraments. The priest or bishop often prayed spontaneously as he celebrated. One can see advantages in such celebrations: they could be more alive, more personal, or more meaningful. But there were also disadvantages. Some people can easily get stuck for words, especially in public; others can be intolerably long-winded. The result could be that the meaning of the celebration might be obscured for people. Quite soon, about 200 CE, Church leaders began to write down the order of things to be done and the words to be said.

Gestures also were added. Some like elevated hands were ancient biblical ones (see 1 Tim 2:8). Others, like hands being joined, were from converted Germanic peoples. The result of both words and actions was ritual and a recognised, and later an approved way, of celebrating. All the main Christian Churches have ritual or ordering for their sacraments.

We should evaluate ritual positively. It has a guaranteed meaning and efficacy. We do not leave the Church saying, 'I wonder if I am really confirmed.' If the ritual is properly followed, then we can be sure that Christ through his Spirit has touched our lives. But there can be a problem of ritualism, especially in sacraments, which are frequently celebrated, like the Mass. The minister may not be careful, well prepared, dignified or worthy. There can be people attending, but not attentive; they may be physically present, but absent in thought. In general one can say that we must think about a sacrament before its celebration, so that we are alert to what is happening; we need to reflect afterwards so that we can make our own what happened in a brief period of time.

Sacraments in the Roman Catholic Church

We have already noted the seven sacraments that are celebrated in the Roman Catholic Church. This is not the place to give a complete account of any of them, but rather to look at them from the perspective of their symbolism and celebration. It will be helpful to speak briefly about their symbol and effect. The sacraments represent stages in the Christian life and reflect a certain parallel with our natural lives: we are born, grow, and fall ill, all in a community.

Baptism

The first sacrament is *baptism*. It is the sacrament of birth into the Church. Its symbol is water with the words, 'I baptise you in the name of the Father, and of the Son and of the Holy Spirit. Amen.' Water is a symbol with a wide range of meanings. But the words of the sacrament specify the meaning of the washing or immersion (see *Catechism* nn. 1213-1216). Baptise means 'to plunge into'. The person is thus inserted into the name, that is, the Persons of the Father, Son and Spirit. Such an insertion guarantees divine life or grace. It means that everything of sin is removed. Being inserted into the Son allows entry into the Church. The change is so profound that scripture speaks of baptism as 'a new creation' (see Rom 6:3-4). There are many rites which help to bring out the meaning of baptism: welcoming at the church door with the sign of the Cross, scripture readings, prayer against evil, blessing of the water, anointings, a white garment, a lighted candle.

Baptism is also called the door to the other sacraments. The baptismal consecration is such that the sacrament cannot be repeated. No sin can extinguish the sacrament. Except for some members of a few Christian bodies like the Society of Friends and the Salvation Army, all Churches celebrate baptism and there is widespread mutual recognition of the sacrament. It is the basis for membership of the common Christian family in which we are all brothers and sisters in Christ (see Rom 8:29).

Confirmation

The second initiation sacrament is *confirmation* (called in the Eastern Churches, *chrismation*). The two names bring together the main truth about the sacrament: it is about strengthening (confirmation) and about anointing with sacred oil (chrismation). The sacramental sign is an amounting with the oil of chrism (called in the East myron) which is perfumed olive oil and must be blessed by a bishop. The person is anointed on the forehead (and on other parts of the body in the Eastern Churches) with the words, 'Be sealed with the Gift of the Holy Spirit' or in the East, 'The seal of the gift that is the Holy Spirit.' The symbol also includes the minister, usually a bishop in the West, but a priest in the East, the recipient and other members of the Church.

The meaning of the sacrament is that of strengthening or being further empowered to serve and witness in the Church. The person is said to be given the Holy Spirit who will henceforth be a source of comfort and strength for the Christian life (see *Catechism* 1302-1305). Other rites reinforce this meaning: scripture readings recalling the coming of the Holy Spirit at Pentecost or at other times in the Church, renewal of the promises of baptism, profession of faith, prayer for the Spirit and intercessions for future fidelity on the part of those confirmed.

Eucharist

The third sacrament, the *Eucharist,* is the central sacrament of the Church; indeed some would say its very centre. It has many names in the Catholic and other Churches: *Eucharist* for it is thanksgiving; The *Lord's Supper* as it re-enacts Jesus' last meal and looks forward to the wedding of the Lamb (see 1 Cor 11:20; Rev 19:9); *The Breaking of Bread* as the action of Jesus by which his disciples recognise him (see Luke 24:13-35); *The Eucharistic Assembly* (in the East *Synaxis*) for it is the visible assembly of the Church; *The Holy Sacrifice* since it makes present the one sacrifice of Christ; in the East *The Holy Liturgy* for it is the centre of the Church's worship, indeed its being; *Holy Mass* from the words which concluded it, *missio* or sending forth of the people (see *Catechism* 1329-1332). Each of these names opens up one or more elements of the celebration.

The Eucharist is a re-enactment in symbol of the Last Supper, which Jesus celebrated with his disciples. This meal, just before he died for sin was a paschal type, celebrated just as the Jews were partaking of their Passover. For the Jews it was a celebration focussed on a lamb and on unleavened bread (see Exodus 12:8-11). It was eaten in haste to commemorate the escape from Egypt. For Jesus the centre was bread and wine through which he established a new covenant, through which his followers could find in him the Bread of Life. Earlier he had said:

> Those who eat my flesh and drink my blood have eternal life, and I will raise them up on the last day; for my flesh is true food and my blood true drink. Those who eat my flesh and drink my blood abide in me and I in them. (John 6:54-56)

He fulfils his promise and henceforth the Church celebrates again his words and action:

> Before he was given up to death, a death he freely accepted, he took bread and gave you thanks. He broke the bread, gave it to his disciples, and said: 'Take this, all of you, and eat it: this is my body which will be given up for you'. When supper was ended, he took the cup. Again he gave you thanks and praise, gave the cup to his disciples, and said: 'Take this all of you, and drink from it: this is the cup of my blood, the blood of the new and everlasting covenant. It will be shed for you and for all so that sins may be forgiven. Do this in memory of me.'

(*Eucharistic Prayer II.* See Luke 22:19-20 with parallels and 1 Cor 11:23-26).

The worship of the Jewish community consisted of scripture reading and prayer, and the Christian community soon took over the same structure for its celebration of the Lord's Supper.

Since Vatican II it is customary to speak of two tables at which we are fed: the table of the Word, which teaches; and the table of the sacrament in which we receive the Body and Blood of the Lord and are in communion with him (*Catechism* 1346). The first part, the liturgy of the Word, opens with praise of God and an acknowledgement of sinfulness; it proceeds to prayer and reading from the Word of God from the Old and New Testament that climaxes with the Gospel reading. The president gives a homily or reflection on the Word that has been read, 'for all scripture is inspired by God and is useful for teaching, for reproof, for correction, and for training in holiness, so that everyone who belongs to God may be proficient, equipped for every good work' (2 Tim 3:16-17). Intercessions for the Church and the world then follow. The key symbolism in this part of the celebration is that of a community gathered listening to and instructed and encouraged by the Word and responding in prayer.

The second part of the liturgy focuses on the community gathered around the Lord. There are prayers of preparation and of thanksgiving before the Eucharist Prayer, which re-enacts the Last Supper. The Eucharist Prayer has several key moments: it is addressed to the Father; it asks for the Holy Spirit to sanctify the bread and wine to make them the Body and Blood of the Lord; it commemorates the death and resurrection of Jesus; it joins with the saints in heaven in the praise of God; it asks for the gifts of unity and peace for the Church and it commemorates the dead. This central prayer leads on to the rite of Communion for the assembly.

Vatican II has a saying of the French theologian Henri de Lubac has been widely quoted, 'The Church makes the Eucharist and the Eucharist makes the Church.' The Eucharist is the central sacrament of the Church; in it the Church finds its highest expression. The whole ritual of the Eucharist in all its parts and symbols leads to the understanding of Vatican II, which stated:

> Taking part in the Eucharistic sacrifice, the source and summit of the Christian life, the people offer the divine victim to God and themselves along with it. (*Church*, LG 11)

It is the source of the Christian life, for all that the followers of Jesus treasure is found in his death and resurrection; it is the summit, for being joined to this mystery gives meaning to our whole lives. It is only through the Eucharist that one is fully a Catholic. Hence it is also called a sacrament of initiation.

Reconciliation/penance

We have considered the spiritual life as mirroring human life. Both have times of weakness and illness. The Church has been given sacraments of healing. The main spiritual illness is sin and for this we have the sacrament of *penance*. Again, like the Eucharist, it has several names: *penance* for it consecrates the sinner's conversion and return; it is *confession* – an acknowledgement of sins which are submitted to God for forgiveness through the Church; it is *reconciliation* as it re-establishes relations with God and others, through the act of God.

We know from scripture that Jesus left the power of forgiving sins to his Church (see John 20:21-23). The rites for the exercise of this authority have varied throughout the centuries. In its simplest form it is a meeting of the sinner and a priest. The priest represents Christ, whose power he shares, as well as the Church. People sometimes ask why one needs to confess to a priest: can one not say 'I am sorry to God?' One can indeed, but one may not find reassurance or advice in a lonely prayer. From the priest we hear that we are forgiven, we can get advice about our lives, and we leave with inner peace.

The core symbolism is confession of sin and the words of absolution when the priest says:

> God the Father of mercy through the death and resurrection of his Son has sent the Holy Spirit among us for the forgiveness of sin. Through the ministry of the Church may God give you pardon and peace and I absolve you from your sins in the name of the Father and of the Son and of the Holy Spirit. Amen.

Other rites encircle this core symbolism. The priest welcomes the person approaching the sacrament; there should be phrase or reading from scripture; there is an opportunity for the person to express sorrow for sin; the priest imposes his right hand on or towards the head of the penitent (an invocation of the Holy Spirit); there is a penance – prayer or good work – which is a token of the resolve to amend one's life and to avoid sin. There are also public celebrations of the sacrament in which there can be a more elaborate ritual with readings, hymns, a homily, and intercessions as well as the opportunity for private confession. The whole symbolism of the sacrament revolves around a double truth of the person seeking reconciliation with God and with others, and God reaching out in love and forgiveness.

The Anointing of the Sick

The second healing sacrament is the *anointing of the sick*. This has its foundation in the healing ministry of Jesus and his apostles (see Mark 6:13), and is based on a text of James, which counsels prayer and anointing for the sick (Jas 5:14-15). The core symbolism is laying on of hands, which liturgically is a prayer for the Holy Spirit, and anointing with blessed oil on the forehead and hands with the words:

> Through this holy anointing may the Lord help you with the grace of the Holy Spirit. Amen. May the Lord who frees you from sin save you and raise you up. Amen.

The imposition, or laying on, of hands as well as the anointing draw on the powerful symbolism of touching. There is a sense of caring in this touch with love that is far deeper than anything we might say. There are ancillary rites that complement the symbolism, viz. scripture reading and prayers. All of these communicate the fact that Christ through his Church in the person of the priest, as well as friends or relatives who may be present, is showing compassion for sickness and at work to heal, relieve anxiety, and strengthen the person in body, mind and spirit (see 1 Thess 5:23).

Marriage

The two social sacraments concern the family and the Church as a whole. The first, *marriage,* is concerned with the most basic unit of human society. The core symbolism is the exchange of consent, whereby two free people join with each other to become one (see Matt 19:4-6). Various cultures have their own symbolism for the expression of consent; in Ireland it is made explicit with the words: 'Do you take [name] as your wedded husband/wife? I do.' There are further symbols such as rings, exchange of tokens; the couple naturally add a kiss to the rite. All of these bring out the meaning of the sacrament. As usual in sacraments there are readings and prayers as well as a homily in order to bring out the significance of the sacrament. The Catholic Church in the West considers the ministers of the sacrament to be the couple, with the priest being an official witness. In the East, where the ceremony is called 'Crowning' the priest who performs this act is seen as the minister. The symbolism of the sacrament is seen to stress God's blessing on the event, as well as joy, love, friendship and the support of the Christian community, relatives and friends.

Orders

The final sacrament is *orders*, which is in three degrees: deacon, priest and bishop. The word used about the rite is 'ordination', which is a rite of blessing, and consecration. By it a person is given a special share in the priesthood of Christ. Ordination is the sacrament that provides ministers for many of the sacred rites of the Church. The core symbolism of the rites for deacon, priest and bishop is an imposition of hands on the head of the person being ordained and a solemn prayer for the Holy Spirit to come upon the person giving them power and authority in the Church. There are scripture readings, prayers and other elements of the rite. In the case of each order the person is clothed in the appropriate liturgical vestments. A priest's hands are anointed and he is given the chalice and paten as symbols of his celebration of Mass. The main symbolism of the sacrament is that of setting the person apart and giving them a role of service in the Church, a service that they are to perform in the name or person of Christ and with his authority.

A characteristic of Roman Catholic sacramental thought is its precision about rites, their meaning and effects, and careful specifications about administration. Other Churches of the East and from the Reform do not have such exactitude, which can lead to misunderstanding when members of different Churches discuss sacrament.

Other Christians: the Anglican Communion

The various Christian Churches have their own rites and understanding of sacraments. The twenty-nine Provinces within the Anglican Communion (not 'The Anglican Church'), such as the Church of Ireland, the Church of England, etc. have liturgical rites that go back to *The Book of Common Prayer* (BCP) that emerged in the reigns of Edward VI (d. 1553) and Elizabeth I (d. 1603). The text and rites draw on more ancient traditions of the Church. The BCP was standardised in 1662, and was largely unchanged until the twentieth century. Earlier exceptions, however, were the Episcopal Church of Scotland, the Episcopal Church of the United States and the Church of Ireland, which began revisions in the nineteenth century. This work of renewal and updating is still going on in Anglicanism. A major revision of the services of the Church of Ireland was published in Spring 2004.[5]

Anglicanism shares with other Churches of the Reform a main focus on the two sacraments most clearly taught by the Lord (the 'Dominical sacraments'), that is, baptism and the Lord's Supper, also called Holy Communion. The leaders of the sixteenth-century Reformation tended to uses scripture as the measure of all Church practice. In some Churches of the Reform this became hardened to a principle of *scriptura sola* (scripture alone), so that what was not clearly seen in the scriptures could not be imposed, and was often in practice eliminated. The Anglican Churches, with their traditions of being Reformed and Catholic, retained in various forms other sacramental rites, but tended to restrict the word 'sacrament' to the two clearly Dominical ones.

Baptism

The core symbolism of *baptism* is common to all Christians. We follow the new BCP of the Church of Ireland. It has two rites for baptism: one more traditional in line with the ancient BCP ('The Ministration of Public Baptism of Infants'), the other a thoroughly revised ceremony 'Holy Baptism Two'. We take the meaning of the sacrament from the second rite. It is the immersion or pouring of water in the name of the Trinity. The BCP does not have any anointing at baptism, though this is permissible in several other services. Great emphasis is placed on the congregation attending the service. The child being baptised is seen as entering the Church, being born anew in the water and being cleansed of all sin. There are several prayers and a reading from scripture. There are some additional symbolic actions: the sponsors renounce evil and profess faith in the name of the child. A sign of the Cross is made on the forehead of the child. The meaning of the rites and symbols, and the effect of the sacrament, do not significantly differ from Roman Catholic understanding of them. The Pastoral Introduction in the BCP reads:

> The service paints many vivid pictures of what happens on the Christian way. There is a sign of the cross, the badge of faith in the Christian journey, which reminds us of Christ's death for us. Our 'drowning' in the water of baptism, where we believe we die to sin and are raised to new life, unites us to Christ's dying and rising, a picture that can be brought home vividly by the way baptism is administered. Water is also a sign of new life; we are born again by water and the Spirit through faith in Jesus Christ. And as a sign of new life, there may be a lighted candle, a picture of the light of Christ conquering the darkness of evil. All who are baptised walk in that light for the rest of their lives.[6]

Roman Catholic theology would add somewhat to this statement, but would agree with what is expressed here.

The Lord's Supper

The celebration of the *Lord's Supper* or *Holy Communion* is central to Anglican worship.[7] It has possible variety, depending on which of the two rites in the new BCP is used. Common to the Lord's Supper in all Christian Churches are bread and wine, and remembrance. This is not any kind of memory; it is making present and effective what has happened in the past. Anglicans and Roman Catholics have come to agreement that the Eucharist is 'a means through which the atoning or saving work of Christ on the Cross is proclaimed and made effective in the Church.'[8] The service of Holy Communion shares many of the elements found in Roman Catholicism, though in a different order and with different language: there is praise of the Father, admission of sin, readings from scripture, intercessions for the Church and society, the Our Father, Creed and Gloria, and recitation of the Lord's words at the Last Supper.

The main difference is found in the meaning of Holy Communion and the status of the holy elements. The faith of Roman Catholics is that they are the Body and Blood of the Lord; Anglicanism is not always so specific. The BCP allows for different understandings of the consecrated bread and wine. Traditionally there are two positions in the Church of Ireland. One, in the Low Church tradition, is called 'Receptionist': the bread and wine received in faith become the Body and Blood of the Lord. Outside the reception in faith, or after the Holy Communion service, they are merely bread and wine. The other view is the High Church position: after the prayers of the priest there is an objective change in the elements of bread and wine, so that one rightly speaks of a Real Presence. Anglicans of either tradition do not pursue speculation much further than Receptionism (a word used only since 1867) or Real Presence. Some Anglican Churches of High Church leaning have reservation of the Sacrament in a side chapel.

Other sacraments
Anglicanism also has the practice of other sacramental or quasi-sacramental rites. *Confirmation* is described in the new BCP in the suggested address of the bishop:

> The Candidates will profess their faith in Christ, confirming their desire to serve God throughout their lives, to turn to Christ and to renounce all evil. Then, as bishop, I will lay my hand on them, praying that God's

Spirit will confirm, strengthen and guide them as they strive each day of their lives, to live up to the solemn commitment they make today.[9]

There is much emphasis open the free choice of the person to seek confirmation and on their adequate knowledge of the faith. The rite is seen as a ratification of baptism. As in Roman Catholicism, there is diversity about the meaning and symbolism of the rite.[10] In the Church of Ireland there is no admission to Holy Communion before confirmation – some other Anglican Churches allow it. The use of oil was discontinued in the sixteenth century as well as the sign of the Cross.

There are impressive and extended rites of *ordination*. The title in the BCP allows some different ways of understanding what is taking place: 'The Form and Manner of Making, Ordaining, and Consecrating, of Bishops, Priests, and Deacons according to the Order of the Church of Ireland.'[11] The rites reflect the New Testament institutions of bishop, priest and deacon (see Phil 1:1, and 1-2 Tim *passim*). Each of the rites has a central place for the imposition of hands by the presiding bishop, giving authority for teaching and leading in sacramental and other worship.

The issue of confession *to* a priest has had a somewhat torturous history in Anglicanism. In the BCP mention is made of the power to forgive sins. The main confession of sins is a general and public admission of guilt at the liturgy of Holy Communion and at Morning and Evening Prayer. In the Church of Ireland there is provision for confession and absolution in the 'Ministry to Those who are Sick.'[12]

The Prayer books used in Anglicanism have always had very beautiful rites for the pastor to use in visitation *of the sick*. These concern the spiritual dangers and opportunities that arise when illness comes. The full rite includes the following possibilities and elements: Preparation for Communion; Holy

Communion; Penitence and reconciliation; the Laying on of Hands; Anointing with Oil; Prayers and Readings, and where appropriate, Preparation for Dying.[13]

The Prayer Book also has two services for *marriage*. In prayers and readings they stress the divine origin of matrimony, the fact that it symbolises the mystical union that exists between Christ and his Church, and the need of God's help in mutual support and in the rearing of children. The core symbols are the exchange of vows by the man and woman, and the giving of a ring(s).

Conclusion

This chapter allows a comparison between the sacramental life of the Roman Catholic Church and the Church of Ireland. We can see many points in common both in theology and in ritual. There are also differences, which arise out of centuries of differing theological perspectives. What we should find in examining the liturgical books of the Churches is the beauty of their rites, which should deepen our mutual respect. If a comparison with other Christian Churches, such as Methodist or Presbyterian, had been chosen, then one would be confined to the 'Dominical sacraments', though recognising that there are other important rites in these Churches that are not regarded as sacraments.

Notes

1. *Constitution on the Liturgy*, SC 7 [the internal reference is to the teaching on the Mass by the Council of Trent (1562)].

2. See R. Vereecke 'Gestures, Liturgical' in P.E. Fink, ed., *The New Dictionary of Sacramental Worship* (Dublin: Gill and Macmillan, 1990) pp. 503-513. The matter is also treated in many manuals of liturgy.

3. See *General Instruction for the Roman Missal* n. 234.

4. See *General Instruction for Children's Masses* (1973) nn. 33, 34.

5. *The Book of Common Prayer according to the use of the Church of*

     Ireland (Dublin: Columba, 2004). [Irish BCP]

6.   Irish BCP, p. 357.

7.   W.R. Crockett, 'Holy Communion' in S. Sykes and J. Booty, eds, *The Study of Anglicanism* (London: SPCK/Philadelphia: Fortress 1988) pp. 272-285

8.   *Anglican-Roman Catholic International Commission* (ARCIC, 1971) II, 5.

9.   Irish BCP, p. 382.

10.   See D.R. Holeton, 'Initiation' in *The Study of Anglicanism* pp. 261-272 at 270-271.

11.   Irish BCP, p. 518.

12.   Irish BCP, p. 446.

13.   Irish BCP, pp. 440-456.

Select Bibliography

P. Béguerie and C. Duchesneau, *How to Understand the Sacraments* (London: SCM 1991)

L. Deiss, *The Mass* (Collegeville: Liturgical Press, 1992).

P. Smith, *Teaching Sacraments* (Theology and Life 17. Collegeville: Liturgical Press/Glazier, 1987-1990).

S. Sykes and J. Booty, eds., *The Study of Anglicanism* (London: SPCK, 1988). As noted earlier this book is more focused on the Church of England and United States.

The Book of Common Prayer according to the use of the Church of Ireland (Dublin: Columba, 2004).

Part Two

PRAYER

4

The Need For Reflection

As we begin a consideration of religious experience, we need to examine the notions of experience and reflection. Some of the most ordinary things are hard to describe or explain, like electricity or well-being. St Augustine (d. 430) famously said that he knew what time was, until somebody asked him about it. We can have similar difficulties at the beginning of any course of studies. Not only are there strange words, but also we can find apparently common words being used in a novel way. In this chapter we shall have to look at some ordinary words, which may have a somewhat unfamiliar meaning in the context of worship. As we examine them we shall find that they refer to what we have been doing all along and we may be like M. Jourdain in Molière's play, *Le bourgeois gentilhomme*, who learned with surprise that he had been speaking prose for forty years without realising it.

Experiences

The word 'experience' is hard to nail down. It has the idea of my contact with reality. People sometimes compare book-knowledge to experience, often preferring it to the former. Again, if I open my eyes and see a tree, then the tree, which has been there for years, comes into my range of knowing.

When I take the top off a bottle, I can perceive the scent of a liquid. It was there all along, but the bottle top kept me from contacting the smell. We have five senses or windows through which reality comes to us: sight, smell, taste, touch and hearing. We take these on board as belonging to ourselves. We say quite naturally, '*I* hear the music,' not *my ear* hears; '*I* taste the salt,' not *my mouth* tastes. There is an 'I' at the centre of these sense experiences.

Feelings

There are also feelings that I have. These are various kinds; and various spiritual writers and psychologists speak about them in different ways. There is some general agreement about two kinds of these feelings, which are also called emotions, or passions, especially when they are strong and drive us. The first kind are concerned with what gives pleasure or pain. Let's think of an academic examination. There is an attraction or *love* towards passing. Then we have *desire*: we want to pass. When we pass there is *joy*. The thought of failing gives rise to *hate*, the opposite of love. We turn away from, we are *averse* to failing the examination. If we were to fail we would be filled with *sorrow*. So we have love, desire and joy about what is pleasurable, but hate, aversion and sorrow about what is painful.

There is another way we could think of feelings about an examination. This time we can look at its difficulty. We have *hope* because the examination is difficult, but possible to pass. We have *courage* to keep working; we have to keep studying. Some people *despair*; they give up at the thought of the difficulty. We can have *fear*; maybe we will fail. This feeling can help our survival and the enterprise. Then if a person fails an examination, they will have *anger*, directed against somebody or something. They could be angry with themselves, their parents, teachers, the school, the paper, the system, or perhaps God whom they expected to ensure their success.

We will experience some of these emotions or drives every day of our lives. They are not always strong or easily identifiable. It would be good to try out a few more examples of these feelings in other areas of life, for example, a relationship, a game or match, a festival, or a journey.

Decisions

We can put this human activity another way, again recognising our own experiences. Firstly, there is a sense level by which we are in some direct contact with the external world. Secondly, we wonder about what comes before us and we try to understand what we perceive. We can then move on to weigh things up, decide whether something is true or false. Fourthly, we can be responsible, deciding on various courses of action and making decisions. For example, I am in a town and I see a garment in a shop. Then I wonder what it would be like on me, whether it would fit me, what others would think of my wearing it? I move on to reflect still more. Does it go with any clothes I have? Will I have an occasion to wear it? From seeing the garment on a shop dummy, I can make the judgement that it would look fine on me and that it would be good to buy. But there is a further stage in which I have to be responsible. Can I afford it? Is it too extravagant? Should I use my money on something else or in a better way? Eventually I come to a decision to buy the garment or move quickly away from the shop. This process of perceiving, thinking, judging and deciding may be very quick, or, if the matter is serious, quite protracted.

Communication problems

Our experiences can be about many areas of life. Experiences can be sensory; they can be aesthetic; they can be relational; they may be mystical. A very important feature of experience is the difficulty of communication. Thus we can try to tell a person how we feel by saying 'I am fine /great/ low/ depressed/ anxious/ fearful/ excited /miserable....'

Two friends can have similar experiences at a match or at a concert. They can recall it, share how they felt. But it is extremely difficult to tell somebody who was not at a match or a particular concert what it felt like being there. We run out of meaningful words, or we use words that express our enthusiasm or disgust without communicating the experience itself 'brill', 'awesome', or 'horrendous' may tell the hearer about the way the experience is judged, but it does not communicate what it was like to have been there.

Such language has serious limits. If I have influenza and the other person has had this illness, then my approximate language may be enough to communicate how I feel. If somebody has been abroad and contracted malaria, they may not be able to tell others what it felt like. The experience itself is incommunicable. They can try to communicate by saying that malaria is like a bad 'flu, only worse. If the hearers have had 'flu, they will have some idea of what malaria is like, but they will not experience this illness.

If a person has never been at a rock concert or a chamber music recital, they will not really grasp others telling them of the kind of exhilaration found in these musical experiences. Language is extremely limited when it comes to experience. Poetry can communicate experiences in a way ordinary speech can fail to do. Music, art and symbols make their own contribution to communicating experience.

When it comes to profound experiences the difficulty becomes greater. Some mystics, like St John of the Cross, found poetry to be a better vehicle for their experience than prose. We can think too of the religious verse of the English metaphysical poets, like John Donne (d. 1631) or George Herbert (d. 1633) and more modern poets like Gerard Manley Hopkins (d. 1889) or Patrick Kavanagh (d. 1968). These all found possibilities of expression and communication through the density, paradox, metaphors and imagery of poetry.

At this point we have some idea of the varieties of human experience at the level of sense, feeling and mind. We have some idea that we operate in different ways when we perceive, understand, judge and decide. We can, however, feel isolated, unable to communicate our experience. A friend may often say to us in exasperation, 'you don't understand', when what they may really mean is, 'you do not have my experience.'

Reflection

We have been looking at experiences such as seeing, fearing, thinking or deciding. We do these all the time. Day follows day; there is a continual flux of events. There is, however, a constant 'I' that sees, fears, thinks, decides, etc. Though I am doing all these things and I am quite conscious, I may not name what I am experiencing.

This can be put another way. Though there is a wide world around us, we may not notice things, even though we may sense them by seeing, hearing or touch. I can see a tree, but not notice that the buds are giving way to leaves. How can I miss this reality? Well, I may not particularly care about trees; I may have other things on my mind; I may not have looked long enough at the tree. Teachers know all about inattention and have various techniques to maintain interest or curiosity about a topic.

A question could be asked: are our experiences like a river in constant flux, or have they a goal? Does life just go on from hour to hour and day to day, or does it have a meaning? Is there a unity behind all my experiences? A most important question will involve seeing any particular experience in its proper context.

A word about me. In the whole process of experience and reflection there is an 'I' at the centre. Much could be said about the 'me'. At present there is an important observation to be made about a certain division in the self. We all know nice things about ourselves, our human dignity and generosity; we also know about selfishness. The bible talks about the divided self in terms of the heart. Indeed the prophet Jeremiah says: 'The heart is devious beyond all else, it is perverse – who can understand it?' before going on to give God's answer, 'I the Lord test the mind and search the heart' (Jer 17:9). St Paul knew an inner conflict:

> I do not understand my own actions. For I do not do what I want, but I do the very thing I hate... I do not do the good I want, but the evil I do not want is what I do. (Rom 7:15.19)

Yet despite this tug to evil, we know the fruit of the Holy Spirit in our lives: 'love, joy, peace, patience, kindness, generosity, faithfulness, gentleness and self-control' (Gal 5:22-23). We know that these virtues are present to varying degrees in our own and other people's lives. We have then a mixture of goodness and evil; evil in our lives can mostly be reduced to selfishness. We may not think of ourselves as being selfish. Our family and our friends may spot it more easily than we can. It may be well covered up, so that we can fool ourselves and appear better than we are.

Likewise, we can miss out on the good in our lives. We can be naturally generous without making a big deal of it. It is good, however, to look at the good in our lives, at the gifts and talents we have, not to become proud and boastful, but to be grateful.

In order to appreciate both the selfishness and the beauty of our lives, we need reflection. The word 'reflect' originally meant 'bend back'. I go from myself to the object and then back to myself. Introspection, though it literally means 'to look into', is not a question of looking inside ourselves, but rather becoming aware of our sensing, understanding, judging and deciding. I ask, 'What am I doing? What is going on?' Let us take an experience of anger. I feel very annoyed. My temperature is slightly up, my blood pressure is raised. I can think of little else but what has annoyed me. In this case, what would reflection involve? Firstly, to note that I am angry and perhaps admit it. Secondly, reflection will enable me to understand it. I am hopping mad because a friend promised to do something for me and has let me down. I ask myself 'why?' Did we misunderstand the arrangement? Was my request unreasonable? Has my friend been thoughtless? I can then move to a third stage of judging the situation. I look for more evidence. I may recall that my friend was preoccupied over the last few days; I may remember that my friend was spending more time with somebody else than with me; I think about our friendship and ask if it is really authentic. After weighing up all sorts of ideas, I can come to a decision. It might be positive to let the matter go or to talk to my friend about my hurt and anger. It might even be a decision to break off the relationship, based on a judgement that my supposed friend is not really genuine or worth considering. Here we see reflection at various levels: the experience of the anger; trying to understand it; looking for evidence before making a judgement; then a decision. Afterwards when I have cooled down and some time has elapsed, the whole process may be quite different, as well as its outcome.

That is just an example of one experience. I cannot afford to go through a big process about everything in my life from washing my hair to eating bags of crisps. However, occasionally I may want to think about shampoos or healthy eating. Usually it will not be the act itself, but a wider perspective. Hair washing will then be considered in the wider context of appearance, or crisps within the perspective of health. In this wider context we have shifted horizon. A horizon is as far as we can see. We widen our horizon by climbing higher or by moving to some other place. A key change of horizon is when we move from reflecting on an experience to reflecting on values.

Reflection on values

The first Section of the Leaving Certificate is concerned with values. Here we focus in on a few key aspects, presuming what is covered elsewhere. When we speak about values we are saying that something is good and worth striving for. At the first level we think of something as being good for ourselves. We may contrast values and conclude that the value of enjoying good health is more important than the value of continually tasting and enjoying crisps. When we consider values we are looking at something that we judge to be good. A value is usually more important than what is immediate or what would be nice to do now. I may feel like watching three videos, but the higher value of study and learning may mean that I say 'no' to this immediate pleasure. Again fitness means that I have to do things that are at times less than pleasant, and I have to forego things that would be enjoyable. But if I am committed to the value of fitness, then I will be prepared to do whatever it takes.

There are many kinds, indeed a hierarchy of values. We can think of personal values: health, cultivation of crafts or abilities like music, painting, cooking or football skills. Then there are intellectual values of learning, knowing, understanding. There are moral values of doing good. There are social values of good citizenship. There is the aesthetic value in beauty. There are personal values of love. There are religious values.

The cultivation of values needs dedication. We will not acquire them by fits and starts. What makes the cultivation of values more challenging is the fact that the higher values demand self-transcendence, that is, aiming at what is higher than myself. It will involve going against an immediate pleasure and being prepared to put up with some negative discomfort or activity. A sign of maturity is the fact that a person will not seek immediate gratification, but will act in a way that cultivates a higher value. In the end we can be sources of evil or selfishness, or we can be principles of benevolence, capable of collaboration with others and of true love.

Values are found in the community in which I live. My family has values, things that it regards as important and which each member is expected to share and contribute towards. Such family values might be caring for others, pulling together, honesty, truth, being good neighbours, etc. The school has values which teachers and pupils are expected to uphold. Society has values. We may not enjoy every moment of the search for a value or values, but we later realise how good these values are for others and ourselves.

The supreme touchstone of values is religion; all religions have their values. The Christian value is to love like Jesus Christ and according to his teaching. For Moslems the highest value is submission to Allah, surrender without conditions to the divine will. Buddhists seek enlightenment. Judaism seeks obedience to God in worship and in the life of society. Religious values demand self-transcendence, moving beyond ourselves to a higher good. Religions offer a meaningful existence in which people will serve God and be a principle of good for others.

The need for reflection

We have been looking at the complex being that we are. We have all kinds of experiences. We have an ambiguity in our hearts and behaviour. We know that we should cultivate values rather than seek immediate gratification.

My reflection is not a lonely or isolated activity. I do not have to start from scratch in being a good person. There is an inherited wisdom in the community and especially in religion that will give me sure guidance for the broad picture of my life, and for many of the smaller dreams, values and decisions. Reflection is necessary for us for quite a number of reasons.

Firstly, we are surrounded by so much activity, by so much noise and information that we need moments of quiet, to think about ourselves, about others, about life and the great questions of our society. We might think of ourselves as taking stock. We cannot just drift like a stick in a river, with one day following the next. The stick will float quietly on smooth waters; it will also meet eddies, go down cascades, get momentarily caught on rocks or by overhanging branches. Its progression along a stretch of river may not be smooth. We need to see the patterns of our lives. We can ask, 'What holds us back and frustrates us?' We need to reflect on difficulties in our lives. Sometimes we will have to wonder how these may be overcome; at other times we can perhaps ignore the difficulty and decide that the problem is only minor.

Secondly, we need to reflect on the direction of our lives. Here we can ask what our desires are, and in particular what our deepest desire might be? These desires will be values – personal, intellectual, moral, social or religious. Further reflection will allow us to grasp how we are reaching our values. We can understand what blocks our search for values, what facilitates and makes these values real.

Thirdly, reflection will lead to the question of what kind of person I am. Am I a good person who contributes to the welfare of my family, of my school, of the environment, or am I selfish, too much concerned with what immediately suits me?

Fourthly, I look to the future. All this necessary reflection can be within the narrow horizon of my daily life. But by imagination I can broaden my horizon. I can ask, what do I want to be like, to be in a few years time? I can dream about my future. Such dreaming has to be realistic, and when I have a significant view of my future, I must be prepared to take steps to bring it about.

Fifthly, reflection must not be merely about myself. We use the word 'narcissism' about a concern for ourselves that is selfish and shallow. Reflection is about my whole self, and that includes my relationships with others.

Sixthly, reflection is needed about some ultimate issues for which there are no easy answers. We look at our world and see so much that is good and beautiful, as well as what is evil and ugly. The Second Vatican Council (1962-1965) summed up profound issues:

> Nevertheless, in the face of modern developments there is a growing body of people who are asking the most fundamental of all questions or are glimpsing them with keener insight: What is humanity? What is the meaning of suffering, evil, death, which have not been eliminated by all this progress? What is the purpose of these achievements, purchased at so high a price? What can people contribute to society? What can they expect from it? What happens after this earthly life is over (*Church in the Modern World*, GS 10).

The most profound answers to these deep questions are to be found in religion. Religion offers 'salvation' which is some cure for the fragmented state in which we are. If offers healing for guilt, a way of coping with failure, a meaning – albeit incomplete – in the face of these probing issues.

Religious experience

The human person at his or her most authentic seeks salvation. Our modern world offers many ways of dealing with the deepest questions. Some, like drugs, are an offer of escape for a time. But the questions will not go away. Again, much advertising is an offer of a pseudo-salvation, 'buy this, wear that, try some diet or therapy and your life will change.' Glamorous photographs, sexual imagery, and appeals to pride or fulfilment underscore that we are being offered something better for ourselves than we presently experience.

The deeper answers are to be found in religion. Religion is concerned with our relationship with the Absolute, whom the Christians call God. This Absolute is beyond us, and we can only reach it by some self-transcendence, that is by reaching out beyond myself, or allowing myself to be brought there. The most basic religious truth is simple: God is; I am a creature. Religion is about belief in, and relating to, the Absolute. Christians believe in God's love: God's love has been poured out into our hearts through the Holy Spirit (see Rom 5:5). As a result we are to love God with the whole of our being and to love others unselfishly (see Mark 12:30-31).

Religious experience is to be found in my relationship with God, the Absolute of my life. It is not a matter of peak moments that draw me out of myself, but of my full humanity in a living relationship with God. At many times I may not notice the God in my life. God may be experienced in a restless pull of my being towards something that I cannot really articulate, but which would make me a better person. God may speak through a sense of guilt, which enables me to recognise wrongdoing and a desire to avoid it. Deeper still is the experience of being inadequate or incomplete as a human being, or of needing some healing or salvation. Whenever I am drawn beyond myself, or I see new meanings and possibilities for my life, God may be seen to be at work through the Holy Spirit.

Religious experience is concerned with my relationship with God. It arises out of my personal experiences of being in need, of failing, of desiring what is beyond me, of guilt, of fear, of hope, of my thoughts on suffering, evil, death. Through religious experience I seek salvation. I may also want to express my wonder at God, my sense of glory and worship.

Fixing some important ideas
We have been considering reflection and experience in a general way. Now we need to hold these examples and try to grasp some meanings. They are words whose meaning is hard to fix. We will not be able to get their meaning in a dictionary, but only from watching carefully the way in which they are used by a particular author.

The Mystery

The German scholar Rudolf Otto (d. 1937) wrote a very influential book, *The Idea of the Holy*, in which he detected in religions 'the numinous' (Latin *numen*, divinity). He had coined this word to catch an experience in religion, which has two aspects. The Mystery is awe inspiring (*tremendum*) and can involve our sense of relative nothingness. At the same time the Mystery draws and fascinates us (*fascinans*).

Experience

Another word that is difficult is 'experience'. The Irish theologian, Dermot Lane, notes:

> The appeal to experience has become so commonplace that it is now in danger of becoming vacuous. The word 'experience' is, to say the least, a rather slippery one. It can be made to mean just about anything one wishes it to mean. If experience is to become a genuine source of theology in the light of Scripture, tradition and the authority of the Church community, then there is a pressing need for precision in the use we make of and the meaning we attach to experience.[1]

We will not be using the word 'experience' in a restricted sense indicating some heightened feeling or emotional state, or merely what we perceive by the senses of seeing, touch, hearing, etc. Lane usefully points to the fact that experience involves some kind of encounter: experience comes about when I and a reality meet.[2] But this meeting has interaction; in experience I reflect. An act of experiencing can involve memory: I have had similar experiences before. It can involve understanding: what is going on? I will generally have an evaluation: is it good or bad? Some experiences are judged in the light of community wisdom: I will have learned that arguing with somebody drunk is pointless, that jokes are inappropriate when there is profound personal distress, etc.

There are many kinds of experience. There are the ordinary experiences of day-to-day living. There are also other experiences variously called 'extraordinary', 'inner' or 'depth-experience'. With Lane, we will use the third; it indicates an experience that brings us into a new awareness of values or truth. This experience most often will not have a different way of feeling (the so-called altered state of consciousness that people can have with drugs, high emotion, etc.). It may be just an 'Ah!' moment. It may be a moment when I go deeper, go beyond what surrounds me. Thus, I can study for an examination; study has its ups and downs. But I can occasionally glimpse that it is really important and I see new worth and beauty in the subject I am studying. Such a depth experience can lead to a new commitment to work, as well as a new tranquillity. People will speak too of 'spiritual experience' which is not easy to describe, but can be the result of the choices we make in living out our deepest values, our basic life choice, what unites us in our striving.[3]

Religious experience

A most difficult phrase is 'religious experience'. Here we find scholars who are primarily interested in some peak, or out-of-the ordinary experiences. Some names we find in reading about this area are William James who studied religious experience from the point of view of an observer.[4] Two other names are frequently met in this area, Alister Hardy and David Hay. They too saw religious experience as exceptional, e.g. a deep sense of God's presence, or being given some unusual sense of the sacred.

It would seem preferable to see religious experience as a depth experience that draws a person to God, the Holy One, the Transcendent One. Reaching out in this way goes beyond experiences like waiting for a bus, buying sweets or watching the news. Lane is careful to point out that 'every religious experience is always a depth experience, though not every depth-experience is a religious experience.'[5] I can feel deeply touched, almost drawn out of myself by music, by the beauty of a sunset, by seeing a mother's love on the street or in a shop. These can be profound depth experiences. But they may not be religious experiences, though they might, if we continue to ponder, lead to a religious experience as we are drawn beyond ourselves to God or the Absolute.

The sense of being attracted to, drawn to, the Absolute is common in various religions. Christian revelation will name more precisely what is involved. God seeks me, before ever I seek God. God's love surrounds me, even when I am unaware or disdainful of divine mercy and love. In other words, God has already taken the initiative in loving and in seeking me out. Religious experience at one level may be seen as my awakening to a relationship that already existed: God loving me. Religious experience seeks to make this relationship reciprocal.

Religious experience is neither an immediate union with God, nor a direct experience of God, that is for the next life. There is a consistent theme in the Bible that no one can see God and live (see 1 Tim 6:16 and texts like Judges 6:22; Exod 33:20-23). We experience God in symbols, in his word, in the effects of his grace. The saints of the Eastern Churches had a saying, 'creation is an open book to those who love God'. We can come to a deep experience of God by looking at nature: a landscape, an insect, or the stars. Religious experience can alert us to the reality of God's presence. A sister once asked the late Irish theologian, Fr John Hyde, SJ how she could get into the presence of God. He answered, 'How did you get out of it?' God is present everywhere; we may not be aware of this presence, which is sustaining all of creation.

Interpreting religious experience can raise difficulties. We need more than the experience. If I am struck by God's beauty, by my need of help, by the sight of suffering, it will be my faith that will enlighten me about God and Providence. I am a rational person, so religious experience should not contradict reason or ethics. It may, however, go beyond what science and human wisdom can fathom. I may not be able to express my wonder of God; I may be amazed at the love people can show, even think them exaggerated; the highest love is beyond but not contradicting reason. I am also a religious person, so my religious experience must conform to faith, especially the revelation in the Bible. An experience of a fourth person of the Trinity would have to be declared objectively inauthentic no matter how vivid it may have seemed. Finally, for Christians, and for believers in other faiths, authentic religious experience will be judged by the standards of the community of faith and by the fruits seen in life (see Matt 7:16-18).

Religious experience is not confined to emotions or feelings. I may indeed have feelings of delight, even of disgust at prayer, but I am more than my feelings. Genuine religious experience must also include knowing and willing or desiring, and these are not emotions.

Religious experience as such is not scientifically verifiable. If I am at prayer or in religious reflection, it may be possible to hook me up to complex machines and to detect what part of my brain is operating. But these scientific tests cannot show whether I am in contact with the Absolute or not. They cannot detect knowledge of the Absolute or a person's taking hold of or surrendering to values.

Religious experience is not always to be evaluated in terms of immediacy. People can go within, or seek spiritual paths, so that they feel that they are passing over a threshold to reach some deeper reality. Religious experience can have such a threshold dimension, but it is neither essential, nor necessarily healthy. Religious experience in the Christian, Jewish and Islamic sense has a dimension of an 'I' who meets a divine transcendent 'You'. A very important aspect of religious experience is searching or seeking rather than touching. An experience in which we seem to transcend reality, go beyond what is material, may be spiritual, but not properly religious for the Abrahamic religions, that is those which have Abraham for Father, viz. Judaism, Christianity, Islam.

Christian understanding

What then is a religious experience? It is what goes on in me, when with some personal truth I reach towards God or the Absolute. That reaching towards is already establishing a relationship between God and me. We need to be careful to use some phrase like 'reaching towards' as a person may feel very dry, very alienated, sensing darkness of spirit, yet search for and cry out to God. Jesus on the Cross felt profoundly in his humanity that God had left him and cried out the words of the Psalm 'My God, my God why have you forsaken me?' (Mark 15:34; see Ps 22:1). Such prayers were common in the Old Testament, e.g. 'O Lord, why do you cast me off? Why do you hide your face from me?' (Ps 88:14).

For the Christian religious experience is always a gift. We cannot even think about approaching God except for grace and God's help. We may not be aware of this grace, just as we may be helped by the vitamins and protein in some food without any understanding of the biochemistry involved.

We can approach the Christian notion of religious experience by considering some New Testament word usage. There is an ordinary word 'to know'(*ginôskô*) which can mean to have information about a person or a thing. There is a word meaning 'to understand' (*synimi*) which implies that we have an intellectual grasp of the person or thing. But there is also a strong use of the word 'to know' which is used of the mutual knowledge in marriage – including sexual intercourse – as well as a knowledge that answers the deepest desires of the human heart. The first sense is found in texts like knowing the seasons and crops (see Matt 24:32); the second is used about Mary and Joseph not grasping what Jesus meant when he spoke of his

Father in the temple (see Luke 2:50), or about those who heard
the parables but did not understand them (see Matt
13:19.23.51). We find the third, strong meaning in texts like
'You will know the truth and the truth will make you free'
(John 8:32); 'the surpassing worth of knowing Christ Jesus...
that I might know Christ and the power of his resurrection'
(Phil 3:10). Such texts and ones used about sexual intercourse
(see Matt 1:25; Luke 1:34) indicate a knowing that is not merely
a matter of the intelligence ('I know the binomial theorem in
algebra'), or perhaps the memory ('I know Killarney'), but is
one that involves the whole person at different levels. Unlike
scientific or geographical knowledge, the third form of
knowing is not tidy or limited; I can grow in knowing a person.
Knowing the mystery of God is a task for one's whole life,
indeed for eternity.

The strong sense of biblical knowing can be seen also in
terms of faith. Faith has two components: an objective
dimension, what is believed; and a subjective dimension, the act
of faith. Thus the objective side is a reality, e.g. Jesus Christ is
both God and man. The subjective side is the act of the believer
who accepts that this is true. The two dimensions are united in
the believer.

But there is more. People not only accept a substantial
number of statements as true, e.g. sacraments, Trinity,
redemption, and so on, but they form their lives around these
truths. We can hear phrases like 'she or he has lost the faith'.
This does not mean that the persons have forgotten the Creed,
but rather something like the fact that they do not follow a faith
pattern in their lives, or that they no longer have a living faith.
Faith is a religious experience in which a person adheres not
only in accepting truths, but also is obedient to the One who
reveals. We can thus say that Christian experience is a
continuous faith experience: it is the experience of faith; it is the
experience that is faith. Religious experience involves a
relationship. When Francis wrote in his *Hymn of Praise* (st. 4),

'You are Wisdom', he was attesting his religious experience. If we say, 'God is wisdom', we may only be making a faith statement.

Conclusion

We have been examining experience, values and reflection. Thus far we have been looking at these as they affect us as humans. But there is another dimension of human life, which is religion. We have already considered the need for self-transcendence, going beyond selfishness and what appears as immediately good or pleasant to us. We only become really authentic when we go beyond ourselves, and refuse to be locked in the horizon of our own feelings, ideas and desires. We can also say that we are only authentic when we are in love. This love is of a special kind, which is not so much about what we gain, but what we offer of ourselves to others. It is the love that Christians call *agapê*, the love by which we can lay down our lives.

For the Christian as well as followers of the other Abrahamic faiths (Judaism and Islam), religious experience cannot be reduced to spiritual experience, because the source of genuine religious experience for them is God who has revealed himself. For these religions it is not any Absolute but the One who is revealed. Christians, Jews or Moslems do not make God in their own likeness or according to their preferences. In these religions faith is the basis of religious experience. Moreover, religious experience reflects the history of God's self-revelation. For these faiths religious experience is not confined to what I feel within myself. Genuine religious experience involves going out of myself – in a word, transcendence.

The normative and highest religious experience is found in prayer in its many kinds.

To this topic we now turn.

Notes

1. D. Lane, *The Experience of God: An Invitation to Do Theology* (Dublin: Veritas, revised ed. 2003) pp. 18-19. The whole first chapter (pp. 16-45) is a valuable treatment of religious experience.
2. For what follows see fine treatment in Lane, pp. 23-45.
3. See B. Flanagan, *The Spirit of the City: Voices from Dublin's Liberties* (Dublin: Veritas, 1999) pp. 4-9.
4. *The Varieties of Religious Experience* first published 1902; many editions e.g. Penguin Books, 1985.
5. Lane, *The Experience of God*, p. 25.

Select Bibliography

D. Lane, *The Experience of God: An Invitation to Do Theology* (Dublin: Veritas, revised ed. 2003).

5

The Human Being As Pray-er

Wherever we have religion, there is prayer. It is prayer that establishes the fundamental relationship between the Transcendent and the person who prays. Usually the transcendent is seen as God or belonging to the sphere of God/gods. An apparent exception may be Buddhism which is not theistic, but in which nonetheless persons praying seek what is presently beyond them, the final blessedness achieved by the Buddha.

For this part of the syllabus one should take careful note of the fourth part of the *Catechism of the Catholic Church,* which was very well received when it appeared; it is comprehensive and very rich.

The one who prays

The person who prays is stating that God is supreme, that God blesses, and that God is to be worshipped. Prayer is most fundamentally a statement about being a creature and in need. Prayer is seeking what religious anthropologists call *salus* (salvation), which is an answer to the great needs of humanity. The Second Vatican Council expresses the needs in the form of questions:

Nevertheless, in the face of the modern development of the world, the number constantly swells of the people who raise the most basic questions or recognize them with a new sharpness: what is the human being? What is this sense of sorrow, of evil, of death, which continues to exist despite so much progress? What purpose have these victories purchased at so high a cost? What can the human being offer to society, what can he expect from it? What follows this earthly life?[1]

In our society we are offered *salus* in empty forms: all advertising is a promise that our life will be better, somehow transformed if we eat or drink something new or special, wear eye-catching clothes, travel to some glamorous place, or drive an alluring car. But no matter how much we may achieve or possess, these basic questions still remain.

Three biblical prayers

The Judaeo-Christian bible abounds with prayers. We take three as examples of those in need. In the book of Samuel we find Hannah praying in her distress at being childless (1 Sam 1:10-17). The bible tells us 'she was deeply distressed and prayed to the Lord, and wept bitterly.' The priest Eli looked at her, and seeing her mouth, he presumed that she was drunk and told her so. Hannah replied,

> No, my lord, I am a woman deeply troubled; I have drunk neither wine nor strong drink, but I have been pouring out my soul before the Lord. Do not regard your servant as a worthless woman, for I have been speaking out of my great anxiety and vexation all this time.

Eli then said, 'Go in peace; the God of Israel grant the petition you have made to him.' This prayer of Hannah is deeply personal.

A second example is the prayer ascribed to David. David had committed two great sins. He had committed adultery with Bathsheba and to compound it arranged to have her husband Uriah killed (2 Sam 11:1-21). The prophet Nathan taxed David with his sin and he repented (2 Sam 12:1-13). The psalm, which expresses the king's repentance, is seen as a model for all such prayer. David asks for God's mercy:

> Have mercy on me, O God,
> according to your steadfast love;
> according to your abundant mercy blot out my
> transgressions.

He admits that he has sinned against God, and asks to be cleansed from it: he knows that God has a right to punish him:

> Wash me thoroughly from my iniquity,
> and cleanse me from my sin.
> For I know my transgressions,
> and my sin is ever before me.
> Against you, you alone, have I sinned,
> and done what is evil in your sight
> so that you are justified in your sentence
> and blameless when you pass judgment.

Sin, however, is a deep problem and David has to be given wisdom to avoid it, his inner being needs to be created anew:

> You desire truth in the inward being;
> therefore teach me wisdom in my secret heart.
> Purge me with hyssop, and I shall be clean;
> wash me, and I shall be whiter than snow…
> Hide your face from my sins,
> and blot out all my iniquities.
> Create in me a clean heart, O God,

> and put a new and right spirit within me.
> Do not cast me away from your presence,
> and do not take your holy spirit from me.

He looks forward to restoration and then he, in his turn, will warn others about sin; he will praise God:

> Restore to me the joy of your salvation,
> and sustain in me a willing spirit.
> Then I will teach transgressors your ways,
> and sinners will return to you;...
> and my tongue will sing aloud of your deliverance.
> O Lord, open my lips,
> and my mouth will declare your praise.

David realises that genuine repentance is greater than any ritual sacrifice:

> For you have no delight in sacrifice;
> if I were to give a burnt offering,
> you would not be pleased.
> The sacrifice acceptable to God is a broken spirit;
> a broken and contrite heart, O God, you will not despise.
> (Ps 51)

At a completely different remove, we have the prayer of Jesus, the sinless one. He had celebrated the Last Supper, which was a ritual anticipation of the crucifixion next day. In great distress he goes to a favourite place to pray.

> He came out and went, as was his custom, to the Mount of Olives; and the disciples followed him. When he reached the place, he said to them, 'Pray that you may not come into the time of trial.'

He wanted his disciples to support him in prayer; even in this time of his own personal crisis he was concerned for them too.

> Then he withdrew from them about a stone's throw, knelt down, and prayed, 'Father, if you are willing, remove this cup from me; yet, not my will but yours be done.' Then an angel from heaven appeared to him and gave him strength. In his anguish he prayed more earnestly, and his sweat became like great drops of blood falling down on the ground.

Luke uses a special word for Jesus ending his prayer, 'he got up.' The Greek word has the idea of being raised up, healed, or supported; nevertheless he must still endure the passion.

> When he got up from prayer, he came to the disciples and found them sleeping because of grief, and he said to them, 'Why are you sleeping? Get up and pray that you may not come into the time of trial' (Luke 22:39-46).

Luke, as always, is gentle with the disciples' failings: he says they slept for grief. The other evangelists make it clear that the disciples let Jesus down very badly; he wanted them to pray with him, and yet they slept. Thus we have his reproach: 'Simon, are you asleep? Could you not keep awake one hour?' And they did not know how to answer (Mark 14:37.40; see Matt 26:36-45). In this text we see a common human feeling of wanting others to support us in prayer, to be with us in time of trial.

The teaching of Jesus about prayer

In the gospels we have teaching about prayer by example and by words.[2] We know that Jesus frequently went aside to pray. Luke is the most comprehensive gospel on his prayer: at his baptism (3:21), frequently and at night (5:16; 6:12; 11:1), on the mountain of Transfiguration (9:28), in fear and distress (22:41-

44).We have examples of his prayer at the Last Supper when he prayed for his disciples and all his future followers (Jn 17). In his words from the Cross we have the supreme prayer of abandonment to God and of caring for others (see Matt 27:46; Lk 23:34.43.46; Jn 19:26-27; 28.30). His teaching about prayer is mostly found in the Sermon on the Mount: we are to pray with forgiveness (Matt 6:7-14), with confidence and persistence (Matt 7:11; see Luke 11:5-13); with humility (Luke 18:9-14) and like children (Luke 18:15-17).He gave the model of all Christian prayer in the *Our Father* (see Matt 6:9-13; Luke 11:2-4).[3]

What is prayer?

From these biblical examples we can immediately get some idea of what prayer is. All three, Hannah, David and Jesus come to God expressing their deepest need. One can say therefore that prayer is coming before God, as we are to express our situation. Thus prayer can be different from one day to another, from one hour to the next. There are so many situations in which we can find ourselves. The great prayer book of the Hebrew people and of the Christian Church is the book of psalms. The 150 songs embrace the whole of human existence.

- The person is in need, is 'poor' in some sense.
- Hope is not in material things, but is in God.
- The person recalls the past when God has been good to the People or to himself/herself.
- One can therefore give thanks for past favours.
- God helps the person, who again gives thanks.

Not all of these elements may be present in each psalm but several are, especially hope and thanksgiving. We might give some of the varied kinds of prayer in the psalms:

> Protection against enemies (Ps 5)
> Sickness (Ps 6) and in old age (Ps 71)

Feeling abandoned (Ps 88)
Persecution (Pss 26; 17)
Exile (Ps 42)
Observing God's law (Ps 119)
Evil inclinations (Ps 141)
Repentance (Ps 51)
Trust in God (Ps 131)
National lament (Ps 80)
Thanksgiving (Ps 138)
Praise for all creation (Ps 8)
Universal praise, entering temple (Ps 150)

The simple description of prayer, 'coming before God as we are', needs to be developed. The *Catechism of the Catholic Church* gives two of the classic definitions:

> 'Prayer is the raising of one's mind and heart to God, or the requesting of good things from God' (St John Damascene, *c.* 675-749).' For me, prayer is a surge of the heart; it is a simple look turned towards heaven, it is a cry of recognition and of love, embracing both trial and joy (St Thérèse of Lisieux 1873-1897).[4]

One could insert a seemingly innocuous question at this point, who is the God addressed in prayer? There are various views of God, so many that the Jesuit theologian M. P. Gallagher used to say to people who asserted that they did not believe in God, 'What God do you not believe in?' He found that many people rejected a very poor or false idea of God.

In prayer we can find people who think of God as 'Mr Fixit.' Others see God as a tyrant. For others God is like a heavenly *garda* watching out for people who disobey the law. Other people fear God as a judge. For the Christian, God is revealed as Father, though the scriptures leave room also for Mother (see Is 66:13; Ps 131:2); the *Catechism* warns us that God far transcends any idea we have of either fatherhood or motherhood.[5] In Islam Allah is called, 'Most Compassionate, Most Merciful.' Indeed Moslems have ninety-nine names for God beginning with Merciful, Compassionate, Sovereign, Holy, Consummate, Guardian, Masterful and Almighty, and ending with Splendid, Guide, Eternal, Heir, All-Wise and Infinitely Patient. The hundredth name is secret to Allah alone.

In scientific studies of religion as a phenomenon there are three morphologies, or ways of envisaging God: Sky God – transcendent and almighty; Mother Earth – ensuring fertility; Lord of the Animals – provider of food. In these categories the God of the Abrahamic faiths (Judaism, Christianity and Islam) is a sky god.

Prayer will vary according to the person's image of God. Thus the Bhil people in Central India pray in the morning:

> O Giver of Grain, be good to the world for joy today. O Giver of Grain be good to me today. Do not permit any evil befall me. Do not allow that I do any harm to my neighbour. Do not allow grain and clothing to be distant from us. O Giver of Grain be good to the world today, and indeed also to me.

In time of distress they have a prayer: 'O God may such a great evil come not even to my enemies, or to those who do me evil.'[6] The notion of God here is of Mother earth; we note too the universal and compassionate tone of the prayers.

Ways and kinds of prayer

Faith knows different kinds of prayer. They use different descriptive words, but there is an underling reality. Using Christian terminology we can speak about two modes or ways of praying, namely vocal prayer and reflective prayer. Vocal prayer is prayer people say aloud. They often choose words that are laid down in the faith community, or in holy books. There are also prayers composed by the saints and spiritual guides of a tradition. The issue here is that one must try to concentrate on the meaning of the prayer, to make it one's own.[7]

The other main mode of prayer is reflective prayer – that is, meditation or contemplation – which will be the subject of later chapters. In this the worshipper seeks God by reflection, by thinking on God's will and plan, by seeking to surrender to God's way.

These two modes tell us how people pray: by words or by a combination of reflection of thinking and words. The other big distinction is based on what is going on during prayer, on the attitude of the worshipper. Traditionally there are four kinds of prayer; adoration, thanksgiving, satisfaction and petition; in the Catholic tradition these are the four reasons for celebrating Mass. There can be subdivisions or overlap, so that in its fourth part, the *Catechism* speaks of five kinds of prayer: blessing and adoration; petition, intercession, thanksgiving, praise.[8]

Adoration

The prayer of adoration is the one that establishes the relationship of Creator and creature. It can have several dimensions. Strictly speaking, adoration is the prayer that expresses the basic attitude of the human before God. It exalts God's greatness. Adoration says of God, 'Holy, Holy, Holy. is the Lord of hosts, the whole earth is full of his glory.'[9]

In adoration there is also the *prayer of praise*. Praise looks at God for what he is, and gives glory, quite simply beyond anything that God does. With the prayer of praise is wonder and awe: the worshipper looks at God who is all beauty, truth and goodness. Prayer must leave our concerns and focus on God. St Augustine says: 'The mark of a mature Christian is the desire to praise God.' In praise we reach out beyond our selfishness to God. Praise prepares us also to reach towards others.

Thanksgiving

The prayer of thanksgiving acknowledges all that God has done: creation, redemption, and all the works of love. In thanksgiving there is the *prayer of blessing*. The worshipper looks to what God has done and responds to it. The *Catechism* notes:

> In blessing, God's gift and man's acceptance of it are united in dialogue. The prayer of blessing is man's response to God's gifts: because God blesses, the human heart can in return bless the One who is the source of every blessing.[10]

In the Catholic tradition the supreme thanksgiving prayer is the Eucharist, in which the work of salvation is remembered and made active for the believer. The scriptures advocate thanksgiving: 'Give thanks in all circumstances; for this is the will of God in Christ Jesus for you' (1 Thess 5:18) and 'continue steadfastly in prayer, being watchful in it with thanksgiving' (Col 4:2).

Petition

The prayer of petition reflects our needy situation. The Christian prays along with, and reflecting the prayer of Jesus. There are many needs, material as well as spiritual. The model of Christian prayer, which is the Our Father, has several petitions. In the prayer of petition Christians pray for the needs of others. In this they have the example of Abraham who prayed for inhabitants of Sodom (see Gen 18:22-33). Moses too constantly interceded for his people (e.g. Exod 17:8-12); the *Catechism* describes him as a mediator for his people.[11] Intercession for others is an important dimension of prayer: religious people pray for food, for peace, for rulers and for all those in need (e.g. 1 Tim 2:1-3; Rom 13:1).

Satisfaction

Though the *Catechism* places this prayer within petition, there are good reasons for singling it out. All religious are aware of human failure and sin, and the response is to seek for mercy. This mercy is not seen as totally unconditional. Though mercy from God is a gift, we are right to expect it. But God requires that people seek to turn away from sin. So there are two gifts involved. The worshipper seeks the gift of God's mercy; the worshipper also asks for divine help to turn and to refrain from sin.

Prayer as worship

We have already been considering worship in many parts of the syllabus. It concerns the response of the one who encounters God or God's action in their lives. Its highest point is adoration, which sets the parameters of prayer: the Creator and the needy human. The possibility of worship implies both humans who desire a relationship with God and a God who fulfils that desire. Worship may thus be communal, that is, performed with others, or it may be private in the deepest recesses of an individual.

Worship implies reverence towards God and all that is related to the divinity. In an earlier chapter we noted the contribution of Rudolf Otto (1869-1937) to religious phenomenology. He coined a word, 'numinous', for the attraction combined with fear that the divinity evokes; it is *fascinans* and *tremens* – drawing, and at the same time repelling or inviting people to keep a distance. It is non-rational (not 'irrational'); it is the response of the worshipper who feels that the divinity is all-holy so that the human person can only respond with humility and respect. It can include all that is associated with the divinity. Awe is reinforced by a sense of mystery that emerges in sacred writings, rituals, prayers and actions. In the next chapter we will examine sacred places, spaces and times.

Islam is especially noteworthy for its sense of awe and reverence. It has notable respect for the Qur'an, especially any paper which carries its text in Arabic. Pious Moslems when mentioning a fellow Moslem often add, 'May Allah be pleased with him.' When Muhammad is mentioned they may add, 'May Allah's blessing and peace be upon him.'

Prayer as relationship

The prayers that we have already seen all imply a relationship with the divine. The relationship will be based on how we see God. For the Christian God is the One who loves, the One who makes the first approach, the One who is the ground of our being. It will depend on how we see God.

Prayer is about cultivating a relationship. It is not a technique like typing or crochet work. It is an art that can be acquired, like learning how to be sensitive. But it cannot be learned if it is divorced from my life. I am a complex being, with a lot of life experiences, bad and good. It is this complex being that comes to pray. Nothing in my life need be excluded from prayer: all my joys and sorrows, all my achievements, all my sins, all my failures can make up my prayer. In prayer I come into my identity: child of the Father; brother/sister of the Son and Redeemer; accompanied by a faithful friend and supporter in the Spirit. I am never alone. Without prayer it is very difficult to know ourselves in a healthy way, to come into healing and integrity. Selfishness lurks very deep in our being.

The means are not all that important, provided that we are honest and truthful. The model of human relationships is very helpful. Firstly, we make the acquaintance of somebody. Then friendship develops: it involves sharing, leaving time, going apart. Thirdly, we grow in love: we are more prepared to lay down our lives for the other; we are prepared to be put out, to do what is best for the one we love. In time, finally, it is good just to be with the other, in silent communication.

We come then a) to know about God; b) to spend time with God; c) to show our love by action; d) to live in his presence. As in friendship, prayer cannot have a no-go area; prayer will be damaged by any exclusions. Our whole being, our whole situation, is the agenda for our prayer.

The great religions teach firmly that God does not need our prayers. An Islamic scholar writes:

> It should always be borne in mind that God does not need man's prayer, because He is free from all needs. He is only interested in our prosperity and well-being in every sense. When he emphasises the necessity of prayer and charges us with any duty, He means to help us... The benefit which man can derive from Islamic prayer is immeasurable, and the blessing of prayer is beyond imagination.[12]

Christians would concur that it is we who need prayer. They would also agree with five reasons proposed for prayer in Islam:

1. It strengthens belief in the Existence and Goodness of God and transmits this belief into the innermost recesses of man's heart.
2. It enlivens this belief and makes it constructive in the practical course of life.
3. It helps a person to realise his/her natural and instinctive aspirations to greatness and high morality, to excellence and virtuous growth.
4. It purifies the heart and develops the mind, cultivates the conscience and comforts the soul.
5. It fosters the good and decent elements in man and suppresses evil and indecent inclinations.
6. It restrains from shameful and unjust deed.[13]

Cultivating a relationship with God in Christian prayer – the *Our Father*

The *Catechism of the Catholic Church* has a splendid commentary on the *Our Father*.[14] Here we are concerned not with all the dimensions of the prayer, but seeing it as an example of a prayer that shows the cultivation of a relationship with God. The prayer is taught by Jesus; the gospels give us two traditions of the prayer, one somewhat shorter (see Matt 6:9-13; Luke 11:2-4).

The prayer addresses God as 'Father'. This immediately indicates the relationship between the Christian and God: it is familial and loving. Christians see themselves as God's children, and therefore are implicitly adopting certain attitudes. The Father is called 'our', so that it is a common prayer that belongs to many others. Elsewhere in this volume we note the limitations of the apparently masculinity of 'Father'. God is also Mother but beyond any of our thoughts of human parents.[15] The Father is described as 'in heaven'. This is not to indicate a place, nor that God is distant. Indeed God is said to dwell in the community and in the hearts of believers (see 1 Cor 3:16; 6:19). 'In heaven' means rather that God is majestic and our eternal destiny. As used in the Christian Churches, the prayer has seven petitions. The first three are directed towards God; the last four express human needs.

Hallowed be Thy name

This includes a prayer that the worshipper wants God's name (a biblical word for 'person') to be made holy throughout the world. It is also a prayer that God's plan of salvation be operative everywhere, especially for those in worship.

Thy kingdom come

Primarily this petition asks for the final coming of the reign of Christ. The Kingdom is also God's rule over creation and over all peoples. The marks of the kingdom are given in Vatican II as truth and life, holiness and grace, justice, love and peace.[16] The prayer is for these values to be in our world.

Thy will be done on earth as in heaven

The last of the petitions directed towards God's glory. Jesus came to do the will of the Father (see Heb 10:7); his food was to do the will of the One who sent him (see John 4:34). God's will is for the salvation of all humanity (see 1 Tim 2:3-4). It has been revealed that his will for us is to love one another (see John 13:34). By prayer people are to discover the will of God for them in practical situations and to find the strength to do it (see Rom 12:2).

Give us this day our daily bread

The petitions now move to human need, the most basic one being food. It is a prayer for all: 'give us'. The bread is not only material but also spiritual. For the Christian it includes a sharing in the Lord's Supper.

Forgive us our trespasses, as we forgive those who trespass against us

This petition recognises the fact of sin and failure. It is a confident plea for forgiveness. One of the most common Christian prayers is an appeal for mercy. But there is a condition imposed by God and revealed by Jesus Christ: the condition of being forgiven is that we too forgive others. Peter thought that forgiving seven times would be generous, but Jesus by insisting on seventy-seven times was declaring that there could be no limits to forgiveness (Matt 18:21-22). In the parable, which immediately follows, his disciples are told that the consequence of being unforgiving is that they will not be forgiven either (see Matt 18:23-35). Enemies must be loved and forgiven (see Matt 5:43-46). The forgiveness is not externals, but must be from the depth of the heart (see Matt 18:35).

And lead us not into temptation
This petition can be misunderstood. 'God tempts no one' (James 1:13). The prayer is asking that God does not allow the person to go into the way of sin and temptation. It is a confident prayer to resist temptation (see 1 Cor 10:13). Stating this petition is already to take a stand against sin.

But deliver us from evil
In this petition one prays that one is not overcome by the Evil One, the tempter, Satan, the Prince of this world (see Jn 8:4; 14:30). The petition is also a prayer against all evil, physical, psychological and spiritual – past, present and future.

For the kingdom, the power and the glory are yours, now and forever
This final doxology, that is prayer of praise, is found in some early manuscripts of the New Testament and in a first century document the *Didachê*. A form of it is used in the Catholic Mass, shortly after the *Our Father*. Many Christians end the recitation of the *Our Father* with these words. They can be seen as a direct contradiction of Satan who tempted Jesus with kingship, power and glory. The Christian is thus ascribing these to the Father.

Amen
The ratification of prayer in Amen, meaning 'so be it'. It is added to personal prayers and to signify agreement with the prayers of others.

The *Our Father* ultimately is not just a prayer: it is a life programme. Christians have to become this prayer, so that all its elements are fulfilled in them. The prayer, then, establishes all the key relationships with God.

Cultivating a relationship with God in Islamic prayer – the *Salah*

As in Christianity, prayer is integral to a whole life of beliefs and practices. Central is the notion of *'Ibádah'*.[17] People are born as subjects and servants of God/Allah. People turning to Allah with humility and devotion perform an act of *Ibádah*. It includes prayer but also morality, such as respect for parents, speaking truthfully, etc. In Islam every good deed performed to seek the pleasure of Allah is an act of worship. The five pillars of Islam are well known: Witness to one God and Muhammad as his prophet; ritual prayer (*salah*); fasting (*saum*); charity or almsgiving (*zakáh*); pilgrimage (*hajj*). The word *jihad* is often used in too limited a sense: it covers all aspects of religion where there is struggle to obey the commands of God and fulfil religious obligations. An Islamic guidebook notes:

> Islam is an integral whole. It covers all aspects of man's life. The pillars unite all human activities, spiritual and material, individual and collective. The obligatory rituals of *'Ibádah'* make faith (*Iman*) to play a practical and effective role in the human life. *Ibádah* is therefore something positive. It is the means by which the faithful can serve Allah as well as their fellow men.[18]

The daily prayer in Islam is to be said with great reverence; ablutions are necessary to ensure bodily purity. One should dress modestly for prayer and face the Ka'bah in Mecca. The prayers are said five times a day. Bodily gestures, such as raising of the hands, standing, sitting, kneeling and prostrations are accurately prescribed.[19] The word *salah* means 'connection' that is with God. It involves prayers along with bodily gestures of worship. With some variations for different times of the day, the *Salah* is:

> [*Standing*] Allah is the Greatest.
> O Allah, Glorified, Praiseworthy and Blessed is Thy

Name and exalted is Thy Majesty and there is no deity worthy of worship except Thee. I seek refuge in Allah from the rejected Satan. In the Name of Allah, the Beneficent, the Merciful.

Praise be to Allah, Lord of the worlds, The Beneficent, the Merciful.
Master of the Day of Judgement. Thee alone we worship and to Thee alone we turn for help. Guide us in the straight path, the path of those whom You favoured and who did not deserve Thy anger or went astray. (O Allah accept our prayer)

[*The following or any other passage from the Holy Qur'an*]

In the Name of Allah, the Beneficent, the Merciful, say Allah is the one and only God. Allah, upon Whom all depend. He begets not, nor is He begotten and there is nothing which can be compared to Him.

Allah is the Greatest.

[*Profound* bow] Glory to my Lord the Great. [*three times*]

Allah has heard all who praise Him. Our Lord: Praise be to Thee.

[*Prostration*] Glory to my Lord, the Most High. [*Three times*]
All prayers and worship through words, action and sanctity are for Allah only.

Peace be on you, O Prophet.
And mercy of Allah and His blessings.
Peace on us and those who are righteous servants of

Allah.

I bear witness to the fact that there is no deity but Allah.
I bear witness that Muhammad is His slave and messenger.

[*Sitting*] O Allah, exalt Muhammad and the followers of Muhammad
As Thou didst exalt Ibrahim and his followers.
Thou are the Praised, the Glorious.
O Allah, bless Muhammad and his followers,
As Thou hast blest Ibrahim and his followers.
Thou are the praised, the Glorious.
[*Silently*]
O Lord! Make me and my children steadfast in prayer;
O Lord! Accept my prayer. Our Lord! Forgive me,
And my parents and believers on the Day of Judgement.
[*The prayer ends with a salutation of angels to right and left*]
Peace be on you and Allah's blessings [*Twice*][20]

Though it may be temerarious for an outsider to comment on the sacred text of another faith, it seems clear that here, too, in Islam the daily prayers seek to establish a relationship with God. There is an act of faith in Allah alone; the worshipper presents him/herself as surrendered to Allah's way. Mercy and goodness are to be sought only in Him. There are also other prayers commended to the devout Muslim, such as prayer at night. The whole of life is dedicated to God's worship and service. Here are two key words used about prayer. The first is *khushu*, which means devotion or humility. The very act of prostration is a statement that the person praying holds the most precious part of the body, the head, to the ground. The second is *ihsan* which means 'to perfect'. In prayer it signifies according to the Prophet: 'To worship God as if you see him and even though you don't see him, he sees you.' Other key attitudes of prayer include forgiveness and tranquillity. Prayer is the heart of Islam.

Conclusion

It is through examining its prayer that one finds the deepest truth about any faith or Church. Prayer, as we have seen, moulds the attitudes of believers. It must at all times be integrated into life. At times we find strange prayers, or at least ones that we may not find attractive, or even find distorted. A just evaluation of such piety needs an examination not only of its text, but also of the whole life context in which it is used. One should avoid what is false or irrational. But there is less to worry about if a person, who has some prayer forms which may be twisted, also has more orthodox prayers and is living an upright life. It has been said in this context that a smudged window can let through a lot of light.

Finally, all religions insist that prayer be constant. If it is to cultivate a proper relationship with the divine, it cannot be spasmodic. If it is to form and mould people's lives then it must be constant. The Christian bible exhorts: 'Pray without ceasing' (1 Thess 5:17).

Notes

1. *Constitution on the Church in the Modern World* GS 10.
2. *Catechism of the Catholic Church*, nn. 2598-2616.
3. See *Catechism of the Catholic Church*, nn. 2777-2865.
4. *Catechism of the Catholic Church*, n. 2559
5. *Catechism* 239.
6. W. Koppers in *La preghiera*. 3 vols. (Milan: Ancora, 1967) 1:63.
7. *Catechism of the Catholic Church*, nn. 2700-2704.
8. *Catechism*, nn. 2626-2649.
9. See Is 6:3, a prayer used in the Eucharistic liturgies of the Christian Churches.
10. No 2626.
11. Nn. 2574-2577.
12. Hammudah 'Abnd al 'At, *Islam in Focus* (Beltsville, Maryland: Amana Publications, 2002, from 3rd revised ed. 1998) p. 57.
13. *Islam in Focus*, pp. 57-58.
14. Nn. 2777-2863.
15. See *Catechism*, n. 239.

16.   *Constitution on the Church*, LG 36.

17.   *Salah: The Muslim Prayer* (Birmingham: Islamic Dawah Centre International, 2001) p. 2. (This section closely follows the booklet.)

18.   *Salah*, p. 2.

19.   See handbooks such as *A Synopsis of Worship in Islam according to the Doctrine of Iman Malik Bin Anas Al-Asbahi* (Dubai: Department of Islamic Affairs, nd).

20.   *Salah*, pp. 14-25

Select Bibliography

Catechism of the Catholic Church, nn. 2558-2863.

Salah: The Muslim Prayer (Birmingham: Islamic Dawah Centre International, 2001).

J.H. Wright, 'Prayer' in the *New Dictionary of Catholic Spirituality*, ed. M. Downey (Collegeville: Liturgical Press, 1993) pp. 764-775).

6

Contexts For Prayer

The Christian is told to pray at all times (see 1 Thess 5:17). A hoary story still retains a point. A person asked a theologian if they could smoke when praying. The answer was: 'you should not smoke when you are praying, but you can pray when you are smoking.' A person can always pray, in any place, at any time, whilst doing anything. The desert monks used to speak of 'arrow-prayers', that is, short prayers, like a phrase of a psalm shot towards God; an earlier Catholic tradition spoke of 'aspirations' (from Latin, to breathe), prayers that would only take a breath.

Apart from such quasi-spontaneous and informal prayer, there are special contexts, or times and places for prayer. We feel that we can identify an event if we can give place and time. There are special places and times for prayer. In this chapter we shall investigate sacred places mainly in the Christian and Islamic traditions, and then go on to consider sacred time in both faiths.

Space and time

Space is not easy to define. We can say that space is where things are. A person or a cat can be in a room, a horse can be in a field. We can see them. Moreover they fit. We can easily think of objects that do not fit into a space: too many groceries in a plastic bag, a large piece of furniture in a small room; a person may not fit into the space provided by the cloth of a shirt or blouse. We are all familiar with space in these terms. Space becomes more mysterious when we approach astronomy; here the space is unimaginably huge. At a limit point does space end, or is it infinite?

Time is measured in terms of past, present and future. Change occurs in time. We know what an hour is, what a year means. We exist in time. We are happy that we know about it. But did time begin? Will it end?

We have ordinary common-sense ideas of space and time that allow us to go about our business. Theoretical physicists, however, will speak about all kinds of different times and space, which we cannot experience, but which are rational; and they can explain through mathematics deep puzzles of the universe. Unless we have special knowledge in this area, we have to be content to leave it to these scientists, keeping an awareness that in some scientific questions of the universe or creation, we may not have the intellectual tools to grasp what space and time really mean.

Sacred space

A sacred space is some area that has boundaries of some kind. It is different from other spaces. What makes it sacred are the rituals or prayers that are celebrated there, the religious meaning it is given by people. It may not always be considered sacred. A holy mountain is a place of prayer; it can also be good for sheep grazing. A holy river can have profound religious meaning; its waters can also irrigate or be used in a non-sacred ways. Sometimes a sacred space is very impressive, like Mount Sinai, the River Ganges, Croagh Patrick; it may be a great building like the Gothic Cathedrals of Europe, the great mosques of the Middle East. Such sacred spaces produce awe, a sense of wonder and astonishment, a sense that there is something that cannot be seized which calls for respect or reverence. But other sacred places may be quite unimpressive to people outside a religious tradition. I could casually drive over some ground that a local people might regard as sacred.

In the Judaeo-Christian tradition we can see certain sacred spaces. Moses walked unwittingly on a holy mountain, Horeb; he was told to remove his shoes for the ground was holy (see Exod 3:1-6). At the giving of the Ten Commandments except for Moses no person or animals was to approach the mountain under pain of death (see Exod 19; in this chapter because of different traditions the text is not fully clear). We note, however, that God did not dwell on the mountain, but only descended on it (see Exod 19:18). The Tent of Meeting in the desert, places of sacrifice and later the Temple would have many restrictions about who might enter, how far and with elaborate prescriptions of dress, purity and conduct (see Lev cc. 16-17; 21-24. 1 Kgs chs. 6; 8-9).

Why spaces are considered sacred

In the study of religions we find several reasons why a space is considered sacred. Firstly, as in the case of Judaism, God designated Sinai/Horeb as sacred; likewise the temple. Secondly, signs and marvellous events occur which lead people to regard the place as holy. This is especially true if there is a hierophany, a divine appearance (Greek *hieros* – sacred, *phanein* to show), like Bethel (see Gen 35:1-15). Thirdly, places are holy because of religiously significant events that occurred there: the Temple Rock from which Muhammad ascended to heaven, Calvary and the Church of the Holy Sepulchre as the places of Christ's death and resurrection; Lourdes as a place of apparitions of the Virgin Mary. Fourthly, places are sacred because of a holy person having been buried there.

There are four important features of sacred places. Firstly, sacred spaces or places are where communication with the divine occurs. Churches are places where people meet God.

Their architecture may reflect this. The prominence of the pulpit in Reformation Churches reflects that here God's word is proclaimed and explained. Catholic and Eastern Churches traditionally faced East, the rising sun, because Christ is the true Sun, the true light of the world. The tabernacle for reservation of the Blessed Sacrament in Catholic and some Anglican churches is clearly a focus of encounter.

Secondly, they are places where people experience divine power, particularly healing. Many pilgrimage sites, like Lourdes, are places where people seek healing. They are also places where people seek salvation and conversion. In some religions certain initiation rites take place in a special place, a cave or forest. Here the idea of moving from one state of darkness to light or new life is clearly operating.

Thirdly, sacred places reflect the world, but on another plane. A Gothic church represents the Body of Christ (the Church) the apse as the head representing Christ, the nave the trunk of the body; the transepts the limbs. It is, of course, also in the shape of each human body. Such meanings are not simple; other ideas can be superimposed. The sacred area of an Orthodox church, the chancel or reserved area at the top, has been likened to the soul and the altar to the spirit.

Fourthly, sacred places and spaces teach the worshipper. The medieval cathedral had the whole of salvation history in its windows and carvings. The iconostasis, that is, the screen covered with the sacred icons, teaches Eastern Christians at the Divine Liturgy that what they are celebrating belongs most fully to heaven, to the New Jerusalem; the icons remind them of all the heavenly persons. Often sacred words or texts are written on the walls or furnishings of sacred places.

Places of worship

Places of worship go by various names: church or chapel in a Christian context; synagogue for Jews; mosque for Moslems; temple for other faiths. The sacred buildings of all religions need to be interpreted through their beliefs and values, their sacred history and narratives.[1]

There are, however, several features common to all of these. They are a centre of the community. Members of their faith community feel a sense of ownership. It belongs to the people. In parts of Ireland the Catholic church building is called *teach an phobail* (house of the people); elsewhere it is *teach Dé* (house of God). Moreover, once people's subsistence needs of food, warmth and clothing are met, they give generously to provide places for worship. They are generally adorned with art, figures, carvings, and furnishings. The materials of a sacred building are generally what would be expensive for the area and its people. This is of course relative. But a church in a rich urban area will not be less beautiful or elaborate than surrounding buildings. Similarly a simple missionary chapel in an African kraal will be better built than the dwellings surrounding it. There is deep symbolism at work here. People honour the divinity by being generous in the materials used for a sacred building. Moreover, the place of worship is the only beautiful building that the really poor and marginalised can enter and feel at home, sensing that it is theirs.

In addition to formal buildings for worship, people can make their own sacred space. In their own homes people can have a point of focus like a picture or icon. Some people have a little prayer corner in their dwellings. For others a place is made sacred just for the time of prayer by lighting a candle, burning incense or erecting a sacred image.

Christian churches

Christian churches are as varied as Christians. Their architecture and furnishings reflect the religious traditions of the community. It is the place for liturgical worship. The altar is central in churches, which have as their primary celebration the Lord's Supper or Eucharist. In others it is the pulpit. In Catholic churches the Tabernacle is a focus. The treatment of the sacred space at Knock below will cover many of the main features of Christian places of worship, though some of its elements are found only in Catholic churches.

Synagogue

In Hebrew the synagogue is called the *Bet ha-knesset* (assembly house). It is a place of study and learning as well as a place of prayer.[2] The design and style often reflects other religious architecture in an area. The central area for worship focuses on the ark, a large cupboard often richly decorated, which holds the scrolls of the Law, handwritten texts of the Pentateuch or first five books of the Hebrew (and Christian) scripture. The ark is usually at that part of the building nearest to Jerusalem. The text is read continuously at morning service so that it is heard in the course of a year. In the centre of the worship area is the reading desk. People sit along the sides of the area facing inwards towards the desk. In more traditional synagogues, men and women sit apart.

Mosque

The mosque (*masjid*, place of prostration) is the centre of the Muslim community. It is a place where people gather for prayer, for funerals, and weddings. People seek instruction there, and it is a place for community and family events. In a mosque many profound religious truths are taught in its structure and decoration.[3] The mosque faces Mecca, and its interior is focussed on the *mirhab* or prayer niche. This indicates the direction of Mecca and prayers are read from there. But this is kept empty, for God does not dwell there. The Abrahamic religions, that is, descended from Abraham – Judaism, Christianity and Islam – all agree that, while God is the Creator of the world, he transcends it and is not within it. There is an emphasis on the inner purity of the worshipper. There can be provision for ritual washing near its entrance. The building is holy, so that one removes one's shoes. There is an outer courtyard clearly marked off from the holiest area (*haram*). Mosques are often richly decorated with intricate geometrical patterns and flowing latticework. Rich materials, especially marbles and carpets, are common. Verses from the Qur'an are found on the walls. Human figures are avoided. Like the Jewish synagogue, the mosque is also a place for quiet prayer, reflection and study. Mosques have no furniture, as most prayers are said on the ground. There can, however, be a pulpit, *minbar*, moveable or immovable, which is used for sermons, announcements and lectures.

A word about presence

God is outside space and time. So what do we mean by saying that God or a spiritual being is present? It cannot be by the body, as we have seen in the case of a person, a cat or a horse. Spiritual beings do not have bodies. They are said to be present when they are acting. We can say that God is present when he is acting. The Christian, and many other faiths, believe that God is the Creator who sustains all things in being. So God can be said to be present in all creation, because he keeps it in being. Similarly, people say that God is especially present in some place; that means that he is especially active there. It is usually a sacred space or sacred time.

A sacred place: Knock

Any sacred place can be instructive about religious meaning. Take the pilgrimage village in Co Mayo, where there was an apparition in 1879. What follows as a description of a sacred site is accurate, even if one were to hold negative views about the apparition itself. A study of Knock as a sacred place will also provide material for the section of the syllabus that deals with pilgrimage (3.2).[4]

The village of Knock, now happily bypassed, was on the main road from Sligo to Galway, forming with Claremorris and Ballyhaunis a triangle with sides of about 10km. As a shrine it has a central area, which is sacred, and a wider area with facilities such as parking, toilets, landscaped lawns and gardens that provide areas for picnics. On its periphery, but closely associated with the shrine, are the museum of local history, a monastery of Carmelite nuns, the graveyard of the visionaries, and a well-stocked bookshop carrying books that range from the heavily theological to the very popular.

Since Knock is a pilgrimage centre, there are many other features. There is a large chapel of reconciliation, which allows for the sacrament of penance at most times of the day. In this chapel there is also a counselling service for those who bring personal problems to Knock. The area also has a conference room and a prayer centre where people can receive expert guidance on prayer. There are rest and care units for the sick as well as a medical centre also on the demesne.

The largest building in the area is the Basilica. It extends over an acre and can accommodate 10,000 worshippers. It was built in 1976. It is a very impressive place for worship with a large crowd, but otherwise it does not have the intimacy that many people like for prayer. The word 'basilica' primarily means a form of early Roman church architecture. It has come to mean an important church; there are four major basilicas in Rome. The title of basilica is given by the pope to significant churches in various parts of the world. Pope John Paul II gave the church this title in 1979. Another Irish church with the title of basilica is the church on the penitential pilgrim site of Lough Derg.

In the main sacred area, which is a triangle formed by the old church, the basilica and the station hill used for processions, there are notices asking people not to eat, drink or smoke. An obvious reason for these might be litter, but at a deeper level there is an attempt to delineate sacred space, where very secular activities are not allowed. There are also notices around the grounds asking that silence be observed. The space is meant primarily for prayer. Silence creates a sacred space; it also eliminates distractions for other worshippers. By following the traditional 'station' or prayers associated with the pilgrimage, one can obtain a sense of the meaning of the pilgrimage and space.

It begins with a visit to the Blessed Sacrament chapel, which was opened in 1983. Before that pilgrims visited the old church, which was built in 1828, replacing a thatched penal church. It was on the outside of its gable wall that the apparition appeared in 1879. This small parish church is often bustling with people, but it is a place in which people can feel a profound sense of prayer. It has some old stained glass windows and shrines where people may light candles.

Weather permitting – and it does not always – the next exercises are outdoors: going around the Stations of the Cross and saying the full Rosary whilst walking around the outside of the church. These first three exercises, visit, stations and rosary, are already indications that the Knock pilgrimage is firmly centred on Christ. The only prayers that are directly Marian are the Litany of Our Lady and a prayer to Our Lady of Knock. These are said again in the church or at the enclosed area of the gable wall of apparition. The gable wall has statues figuring the elements of the apparition: the Virgin Mary, St Joseph and St John, an altar with a lamb and cross, and angelic figures. This again is a place where people experience a certain tranquillity.

The sacred site of Knock seeks to cater for the spiritual needs and expectations of a huge variety of people. Mass is celebrated many times during the day. Some people like to express their prayer through actions. A popular way in Knock is to light candles. The symbolism of candles, we saw in an earlier chapter to be very polyvalent. People also bring back home blessed water from the shrine. Again holy water has many symbolic meanings: it is a reminder of baptism; it is a sign of purity; it is a means of asking for divine help and protection; it is a sign of entering into a sacred place. The village itself carries out the important function of providing food and accommodation for pilgrims. It also has many gift shops with a great variety of religious goods. Some people find religious help in articles that others might think of as shoddy or sentimental. Those who find such commercialisation distasteful are not compelled to buy anything in the village. But the shops would not be there unless there was a demand. The objects sold in such places, even if kitsch and of no artistic worth, can nonetheless be a window onto the sacred for individuals. In this connection it should be noted that good taste and holiness are not synonymous.

A consideration of what one finds at a very elaborate sacred space like Knock should allow people to see the key characteristics of the sacred in any local church.

Sacred time

A second context for prayer is sacred time. This has quite a number of meanings. In a wide sense we can say that people create sacred time by assigning a period to their prayer. Thus, in the Christian tradition, people are recommended to pray twice daily: in the morning to consecrate the coming day to God and to ask for divine assistance in all its affairs; in the evening to give thanks for what went well and also to acknowledge and repent of any sin or failure that has occurred. In Islam people are to pray five times a day. This worship, as we have seen in a previous chapter, is centred on the sovereignty and mercy of Allah, that is, surrender to his will.

Human situations are also important contexts for prayer. When people experience a special need they tend to pray. Such needs are innumerable: sickness, examinations, interviews and human relationships are just examples of a special context for prayer.

The main meaning for this section of the syllabus is, however, sacred time in a more restricted or formal sense. We have noted above the difficulty in grasping what time means.

We are so immersed in it that we do not have the possibility of stepping aside to examine its nature. St Augustine's comment is famous: 'what is time? If nobody asks me, I know, but if I want to explain it to someone, then I do not know.'[5] In religion we are not concerned with the scientific or philosophical issues about time. In general religion sees time as linear and circular.

Linear time

We can think of time as a line of indefinite length. We can measure it in hours, days, weeks, months, years, centuries and so forth. Events occur in time. What is past is past. We might with some nostalgia perhaps seek to recreate a past time. Perhaps we would like to live again the 1960s. Then we would seek out its music, wear its fashions, and reflect on its personages and events. But it can never return. Even as we might dress in 60s style and listen to its music, the traffic outside is twenty-first century. Farms are different from the 60s. Shops do not stock many of the items or brands that were available then. So to live in the past is make-believe, enjoyable perhaps as a kind of game, but unreal.

We exist in a certain length of linear time. We can never again meet somebody born before 1890; we will never meet anybody born after 2000. In our life's journey we can advance; we slip back; we can recover over years. At a material, physical or psychological level we can see progress or regress over a number of years.

Circular time

Time can also be seen as circular. One year follows another, each with spring, summer, autumn and winter. Even in our own personal lives, which are in linear time, we have markers that recur – birthdays, anniversaries. It is not, however, that we actually relive the past, but we remember in a focused way the time that has passed. On anniversaries, we may also take stock of where we are; we may look to the future. There is a sense in which we make the past event present by recalling it. People can tell stories about the past event. On the more solemn occasions old photographs may be brought out.

Religions operate in linear time, but most powerfully also in circular time. Great religious events are celebrated on a yearly basis. We might note that religions mostly operate in lunar time. It is easy to note the phases of the moon. It took incredible patience and very many years for peoples like the Newgrange tomb-builders or the Aztecs to make accurate solar observations.

Sacred time gives people their religious identity, which is established by sacred rites. The actions and prayers are based on a narrative of sacred history. Circular time allows people of every age to enter into the truths, values or mysteries of their religion.

In earlier chapters we look at symbol and ritual. These are ways in which we can encounter the past and relive its meaning, even though we remain in the present.

Jewish festivals

Judaism has a weekly holy day, the Sabbath (our Saturday). Its origins are seen in God resting on the seventh day (see Gen 2:1-3). It is a day of rest and a day for worship. The strictness of both of these varies within different communities of Judaism.

The Jews celebrate Passover each year; their sacred meal at that time holds together a sense of sharing the desert experience of *c.* 1250 BCE and their present coming together. The ritual of the Passover meal recalls, celebrates and gives thanks for a past event, which still is operative in the Jewish history; without the Exodus Passover, there would be no Judaism. The date of the Passover, the fourteenth day of the month of Nisan, is determined by a combination of solar and lunar time. It occurs after the spring equinox (*c.* 21 March), which is solar time. It is, however, in the week of the first full moon after that date, namely a lunar event. The Christian

Easter is determined in the same way: the first Sunday after the first full moon after 21 March. The Jewish Passover week begins with, and has as its centre, the *Seder* meal during which the story of God's rescue of his people is told again.

Fifty days after the Passover is the *Shavuot*, originally an agricultural festival for the end of the barley festival, but now celebrating the giving of the Law on Sinai.

A solemn day is at the beginning of the Jewish New Year (*Rosh Hashanah*). Ten penitential days then lead to the Day of Atonement (*Yom Kippur*; see Lev ch. 16). It is a time for acknowledging and confessing moral fault.

Christian sacred time

Sacred time for Christians is determined largely by circular time. Though there are some differences between the Churches on celebrations, there is sufficient uniformity so that we can take the Catholic liturgical year as being most complete; other Christian Churches will have variants, usually by omitting certain Catholic feasts.

The basic structure of Christian time is the Sunday, the Lord's Day. Christians note that the Resurrection of Jesus took place on the first day of the week; conveniently this was the day after the Jewish Sabbath, which led to Christian identity. It is observed as early as 51 CE and known as 'the Lord's Day' (see 1 Cor 16:2; see Acts 20:7; Rev 1:10). It was a day for the celebration the Eucharist. The Emperor Constantine effectively made it as day of rest in 321 by closing the law-courts and forbidding craftwork on it. As in Judaism the observances of rest and worship on Sunday vary in Christian Churches.

There are two cycles of feasts in the Christian Churches: Easter and Christmas/Epiphany. The central feast of the Christian year is Easter, falling at the Passover of the Jews. It was celebrated in the first century. By the end of the fourth century the celebration of Good Friday was introduced; it was a commemoration of the Cross of Jesus. About the same time

came Maundy Thursday (from Latin *mandatum,* command).
This is a complex celebration commemorating the Lord's
command in Jn 13:34 to wash one another's feet; it recalls the
Last Supper celebrated by Jesus the night before he suffered; it
was the day on which sinners were reconciled in the early
Church; finally, it became the day for the blessing of oils by the
bishop for his diocese – oil of the sick for anointing, oil of
catechumens used in baptism, and chrism used in
confirmation, consecrations and ordination. With Holy
Thursday we have the 'Sacred Triduum' (from Latin 'three
days'). The third day, Holy Saturday, was originally a day of fast
before Easter. It is a non-liturgical day; the vigil in the evening
more properly belongs to the feast of Easter, which it initiates.

With Easter as the central feast, other celebrations occur
before and after. The previous Sunday recalls the last days in the
life of Jesus and his solemn entry into Jerusalem (Matt 21:1-9).
A period of penance, the forty days of Lent (from Germanic
words for Spring), was a commemoration of the fasting of
Jesus before his mission (see Matt 4:1-2). It is a time for
conversion and begins with a symbolic celebration, Ash
Wednesday, when Catholics wear ashes on their forehead as a
sign of repentance. The ashes are garnered from branches used
on the previous Palm Sunday, thus giving continuity from the
previous year.

In addition to celebrations before Easter, there are
celebrations after the feast. Following the indication of Jesus'
final departure forty days after the resurrection (see Acts 1:3),
the feast of the Ascension occurs. Ten days later the feast of
Pentecost (from Greek *pentêkostê,* 'fiftieth' [day]) is celebrated.
This was an ancient Jewish feast commemorating the giving of
the Law; for Christians it is the commemoration of the coming
of the Holy Spirit (see Acts 2:1), inaugurating the New Law. It
was called Whitsunday (from the white garments those
baptised at Easter wore). Some Eastern Christians observe the
fiftieth day after Easter as the feast of the Most Holy Trinity,

The Sunday after Pentecost is celebrated by the Eastern Orthodox Churches as a feast of All Saints. From the Middle Ages the Catholic Church has observed *Corpus Christi* (Latin, 'Body of Christ') on the Thursday after Trinity Sunday. In the Catholic Church the feasts of the Ascension and Corpus Christi are holy days on which Catholics are to attend Mass; in recent years they are celebrated not on the Thursday, but on the following Sunday.

Within Anglicanism, the following are special feast days in the calendar of *The Book of Common Prayer*: Ash Wednesday, Good Friday, Easter Day, Ascension Day, Whit Sunday.

The Christmas and Epiphany cycle arose partly at least to counteract pagan festivals associated with the winter solstice, which in Rome was reckoned to be 25 December. The feast was the birthday of the unconquered sun (*natalis solis invicti*). Christians avoided suppressing these days of festivity but gave it a different meaning, the birthday of Christ who is the true Light (see John 1:9; 8:12); hence the feast of Christmas (from *Christ* and *Mass*). Associated with it is the Epiphany (Greek *epiphaneia*, appearance) celebrated in the East on 6 January. The 25 December and the 6 January were celebrations of the birth of Christ in various parts of the Roman Empire. The single feast in time became divided: Christmas became the Birthday of Christ in the West and most Churches of the East; the Epiphany became the feast of the Lord's manifestation at his Baptism in the East and his manifestation to the Magi in the West.

From the fourth century the western Church observed a period of penitential preparation called Advent. It comprises the weeks comprising the four Sundays immediately preceding Christmas Day; it can thus be twenty-two to twenty-eight days. The two figures presented in the liturgy of that time are St John the Baptist and the Virgin Mary. It is also a time in which the liturgy relives the long expectation of Israel for its Messiah. In the Roman Catholic Church as well as in Anglican Churches the main scripture read at that time is the book of Isaiah.

There are three other feasts dependent on Christmas celebrated by Orthodox, Roman and Anglican Christians. The birth of John the Baptist is marked on 24 June (see Luke 1:36); it may also originally have been a feast to replace pagan feasts of the Summer solstice. Another feast depending on the Christmas cycles is the Annunciation on 25 March, nine months before the birth of the Lord. A final feast of the cycle is the Presentation of the Lord on 2 February, forty days after his birth (see Luke 2:22 with Lev 12:2-8).

The Christian cycles of Easter and Christmas-Epiphany are times when believers look to the origins of the faith. The narratives for these are found in the Old and New Testaments. They are times of prayer and for reflection on the main faith teachings that surround the story of salvation. In celebrating the Eucharist or Lord's Supper they seek some encounter with the Risen Lord.

In addition to celebrations in these cycles, some Christian Churches celebrate other feasts, commemorating the saints. The first saints to be commemorated were the martyrs, originally with Mass celebrated at their tombs. In times various Churches had their lists of martyrs, later incorporating other holy persons who very venerated usually on the day of their death – in the Irish tradition called 'the day of their resurrection'. In each Christian Church there are feasts that are universal, that is, shared with other Churches, and ones that are more local, or particular to one Christian body. Thus Irish dioceses have their own feasts not celebrated elsewhere, e.g. St Macartan in Clogher (24 March) and St Brendan in Kerry and Clonfert (16 May). Some Anglican Churches have their own celebrations of saints, e.g. the poet George Herbert (in some places 17 February) or Thomas Cranmer (16 October).

Feasts have various levels of solemnity, but very few can displace the observance of Sunday, which is a major weekly feast. The main saints in the Roman calendar in addition to the ones we have mentioned are called 'solemnities' and are: Solemnity of Mary the Mother of God (1 January), St Joseph (19 March), St Patrick (17 March in Ireland), Sts Peter and Paul (29 June), the Assumption of the Blessed Virgin Mary (15 August), All Saints (1 November), Commemoration of the Dead, All Souls (2 November), Immaculate Conception (8 December).

Islamic celebrations

The holy day of Islam is Friday. Moslems are to join in communal prayer in the mosque at noon. The normal prayers for that time of day are said. There is also reading from the Qur'an and two sermons. On Fridays Muslims seek to capture some of the religious spirit of the holy month of Ramadan.

There are two main feasts in the Islamic year. The first is known as *Eid al-Fitr* and takes place at the end of the Ramadan fast. The main Islamic feast is the Breaking of the Fast of Ramadan. The previous month of Ramadan – ninth in the Islamic lunar calendar – is marked by abstaining from eating, drinking, smoking, violence, and engaging in sex from before sunrise to after sunset each day. It is central to Islamic religious life, being the fourth of its five pillars. It is a most social month. Families get up early to have a good breakfast; supper after sunset is usually more elaborate than at other times of the year. The fast of Ramadan is to teach self-awareness, to make people more sympathetic to those less fortunate than themselves. It is above all else a time for God-consciousness. The whole month has a festive character combined with a genuine sense of piety.

The second festival, which is the more prominent, is the culmination of the Hajj (*Eid al-Adha*). It is a lunar feast on the tenth day of the twelfth month of the Islamic calendar. Its focus is sacrificial, recalling the sacrifice of Abraham (the account in the Qur'an is found in a somewhat different version in the Hebrew bible Gen 22:1-14). During the *hajj* there is actual sacrifice. At home those with financial means are expected to sacrifice a ram. Many Moslems give donations to international Islamic bodies that take care of the sacrifice and distribute the meat to the needy.

There are several other celebrations celebrated by a minority, such as one associated with the life of the Prophet, *Maulid al Nabi* (his birth). The month of *Muharram* is celebrated in some places to recall the martyrdom of Muhammad's cousin Ali and his grandson Hussayn: this is a key feast for Shi'ite Moslems, who number about ten percent of Muslims world-wide; Sunni Muslims are the majority. A consequence of following the lunar calendar, which is about eleven days shorter than the solar one, is that feasts in Islam seem to move backwards, so that feasts that are in Summer one year will be in winter about ten years later. They do not therefore have the seasonal character of Christian Christmas and Easter festivals.

Common prayer

Common prayer is found in most religions. Muslims, however, are not absolutely required to pray in common. But it is strongly encouraged, especially on Friday. Common prayer is seen as strengthening social and religious bonds.[6] For prayer with others Christians have the teaching of Jesus: 'Again, truly I tell you, if two of you agree on earth about something you ask, it will be done for you by my Father in heaven. For where two or three are gathered in my name, I am there among them' (Matt 18:19-20). Here we could recall that such a presence is by power, and by acting, Jesus through his Holy Spirit is present by power. The result may be strength, insight, deeper prayer, or support.

There is a general conviction among religious people about the value of praying with others. Families pray together, since it is in the family that the primary communication of religious values should occur. In all sorts of group occasions it is common to ask somebody to voice a prayer on behalf of those gathered, e.g. prayer before meals, before a meeting. Prayers before meals are found in Judaism and in Islam. Classes have common prayer times, and school assemblies. Such common prayer may be liturgical or ritual, being the official prayer of the community; it may be formal in other ways, for example by reading from a standard manual of prayer. Such prayer times may have readings from sacred books. Common prayer may also be spontaneous. There are also prayer groups where people come to share their insights into scripture, sing sacred songs and pray either spontaneously or in silence.

There are several advantages in common prayer. It is sometimes easier for those praying, as there can be less distraction. It develops a sense of community. It is a leveller: before God all are more or less equal as sinners, as surrendering to his will, as responding to his invitation to praise and give thanks. In common prayer we have the support of others. I may feel dulled, but the prayer of others can carry me. Prayer with others reinforces a religious identity; the common prayer expresses common values and the meaning of life-situations for those praying. The prayers of others can teach me about prayer. Finally, in an indirect way common prayer is educative; those praying are reminded about the major religious truths of their faith.

In the next chapter we deal with individual prayer and that will be a place to explain further the differences between private and communal forms of prayer.

Notes

1. See P. Barnes, *World Religions. Into the Classroom* (Dublin: Veritas, 2003).
2. See D. Cohn-Sherbok, *Judaism. Religions of the World* (London: Routledge, 1999) 78-79; M. Braybrooke, *How to Understand Judaism* (London: SCM, 1995), pp. 37-43. More detailed: D. Cohn-Sherbok, *Judaism: History, Belief and Practice* (London: Routledge, 2003), pp. 483-487.
3. J.J. Elias, *Islam. Religions of the World* (London: Routledge, 1999) pp. 68-69 and *passim*.

4.   See D. Flanagan, ed., *The Meaning of Knock* (Dublin: Columba, 1997); M. Walsh, *The Glory of Knock* (Knock: Custodians of the Shrine, 6th ed., 1994).

5.   *Confessions* 11:14,17.

6.   Elias, p. 67.

Select Bibliography

1. For Christian worship there are three very helpful works of reference:

P.E. Fink, ed. *The New Dictionary of Sacramental Worship* (Dublin: Gill and Macmillan, 1990).

C. Jones, G. Wainwright and E. Yarnold, eds., *The Study of Liturgy* (London: SPCK, 1978 and reprints).

J.F. White, *Introduction to Christian Worship* (Nashville: Abingdon, 3rd. ed. 2000).

2. For other faiths:

G. Beckerlegge, ed., *The World Religions Reader* (London: Routledge with The Open University, 1998).

P. Barnes, *World Religions*. Into the Classroom (Dublin: Veritas, 2003)

D. Cohen-Sherbok, *Judaism*. Religions of the World (London: Routledge, 1999).

J.J. Elias, *Islam*. Religions of the World (London: Routledge, 1999).

J. Jomier, *How to Understand Islam* (London: SCM, 1989).

T.W. Lippman, *Understanding Islam: An Introduction to the Muslim World* (Penguin/Mentor, revised 1990).

M. Braybrooke, *How to Understand Judaism* (London: SCM, 1995).

7

The Praying Tradition

In the two previous chapters we have been considering the pray-er and praying, as well as the contexts for prayer. In these we have seen many kinds of prayer. In this chapter we look at various forms of prayer in the Christian tradition as well as some from the Jewish and Islamic heritage. We will also be interested in prayer from the Celtic tradition.

It will be important that we carry on the notion of context for prayer. In the last chapter we were concerned with the basic context of time and place. But there are also the very many contexts of each faith community. Two issues immediately emerge. Firstly, the way that a faith tradition moulds and reflects the prayer of a group; secondly, the great variety of prayer forms within any tradition. In Christian Churches, especially Roman and Anglican, there is a lot of emphasis on an old adage that stresses the mutual interdependence of faith and prayer (*lex orandi lex credendi*). These four words are capable of varying translations and interpretations depending on whether the core norm is seen as prayer or faith; there is nonetheless a core truth that faith and prayer should not be in conflict.

A problem posed: what is a praying tradition?
We might be able to organise the material of this section of the

syllabus by looking at what is involved in the Roman Catholic tradition of prayer. The sources of this Church's prayer are first of all its liturgical books. These are the books that have the rites, readings and prayers for each of the sacraments, for the celebration of the Eucharist, for formal blessings, for funerals, marriages, and many other occasions. These books are translated into many languages, but they are supposed to conform to the primary text, called the *editio typica*, which is in Latin and the norm under which translations are judged and approved.

An important source for prayer is the *Liturgy of the Hours*, formally called the *Divine Office*. This was imposed on clergy and some religious in the past. Now in translation it is recommended to laity and all religious. It consists of two main sections, called 'hours': Morning and Evening Prayer. Each has the same structure:

- Hymn;
- Three psalms or biblical canticles;
- A short scripture reading;
- A New Testament canticle: in the morning the song of Zechariah, called the *Benedictus* (Luke 1:68-79) and in the evening the song of Mary called the *Magnificat* (Luke 1:46-55) The names are from the first words of the Latin text of the songs;
- Intercessions that in structure resemble the Prayer of the Faithful at Mass;
- The *Our Father;*
- Closing blessing.

There are two other shorter hours: one during the day and one as a night prayer. There is also a longer hour, which is composed of a hymn, three psalms and two long readings, one from the scripture and the other from authoritative Christian writers, mostly the saints. This is called 'The Office of Readings', or in monasteries, 'Vigils'.

These liturgical books are only the official books for Roman Catholic prayer. There are in addition many other prayers used by people according to their choice. Our grandparents had large books of prayers and devotions; particularly popular ones were *The Sacred Heart Treasury* and *The St Anthony Treasury.* These were small in format, but ran to about five hundred pages. There were prayers for all occasions. People read some of these prayers during Mass, and others at times of devotion. These two manuals reflected French and Italian piety of the eighteenth and nineteenth century. The language was rather fulsome, rich and to a modern ear over-elaborate and with excessive sentiment. In addition to such devotional manuals, there were leaflets and prayers for various novenas (from Latin *novenus*, nine each), which were nine days usually in preparation for or following some major feast.

In addition there are prayers that are found in various countries and at various times. There is, in the matter of prayer, great variety and choice. Though official prayers are compulsory for specific liturgical acts, other prayers can be freely chosen.

In all of this one can ask, what is the Roman Catholic prayer tradition? It surely has to be traditions, and even then it will be hard to specify.

Official prayers and popular piety

The example of Roman Catholic prayers invites, or even compels us, to look more closely at kinds of prayer, if we are to have reasonable clarity about the syllabus item, 'The Praying Tradition'. We have seen that in faith communities there are official prayers, which are used for gatherings of believers. In an earlier chapter we noted that some structure is needed to preserve reasonable order and to ensure quality in official prayers. There is a problem of people saying these prayers with others, and even more the attention that is needed if one person says a prayer on behalf of those present. These official prayers pass too quickly for people to grasp their full meaning. Although they are prayers of undoubted value and express the kernel of the community's beliefs and values, they may not reflect the situation of a particular worshipper at any one time.

There is a further problem of the language of official prayers. We might remain within the Roman Catholic tradition for the moment, for there the issue is acute. The official prayers are translated from Latin. They are also in many cases of great antiquity. Unlike its daughter language Italian, Latin is very austere and uses a vocabulary of great beauty and depth. When these prayers are translated, even when the English used is reasonably contemporary, it is still a language that is not familiar. Religious language needs to be dignified, but the price can be that it is remote. One could cite at random the three prayers from a Sunday Mass:

> *Opening Prayer*
> Father, guide and protector of your people, grant us an unfailing respect for your name, and keep us always in your love.

> *Prayer over the Gifts*
> Lord receive our offering, and may this sacrifice of praise purify us in mind and heart and make us always eager to serve you.

> *Prayer after Communion*
> Lord you give us the body and blood of your Son to renew your life within us. In your mercy, assure our redemption and bring us to the eternal life we celebrate in this Eucharist. (Twelfth Sunday of the Year)

The words here are apparently common, though we may not use 'unfailing' and 'assure' in ordinary life. But the thought is anything but simple: what is 'unfailing respect for your name'?

(It is not here just a statement against careless use of the divine name in colloquial conversation.) Again, how are people to understand other phrases: 'keep us always in your love', 'our offering', 'sacrifice of praise', 'mind and heart', 'assure our redemption', 'the eternal life we celebrate in this Eucharist'. These prayers are theological gems, but are they spiritually nourishing unless pondered over at length?

From this example we can see the need for other prayer forms that people feel will reflect their current situation, that will reflect their culture and sensibilities, that can be more easily appropriated and made personal.

From the mid-twentieth century the word 'popular piety' has become widespread. As it originates in the Latin countries of Europe and America, we have to take the word 'popular' in its original strong sense, which is 'of the people' (see *popolare-populaire-popular*); it is not popular in the sense of a pop-chart. The phrase 'popular religion' is to be avoided as it has a quasi-technical sense among Marxist writers meaning what belongs to the proletariat rather than institutional religion. A very rich document on popular piety published in the Vatican in 2002 gives a working definition:

> The term 'popular piety' designates those diverse cultic expressions of a private or community nature that in the context of the Christian life, are inspired predominantly not by the Sacred Liturgy but by forms deriving from a particular nation or people or from their culture.[1]

In addition to official prayers, called in this document 'The Sacred Liturgy', faith communities have other prayers, which are of an optional kind. They enable people to deepen their relationship with God, allow faith to influence daily living and to improve their participation in official ritual prayers.

In a faith community we can sometimes know the origin of a prayer formula, e.g. the hymns of John and Charles Wesley, prayers written by saints or ascribed to them. But very often they will be found in anthologies of piety with the simple word 'Anonymous'. That is 'original' in the sense of its author. The other meaning of origin is spiritual, cultural and anthropological. The origin of a prayer formula arises from a culture, from specific human needs, from a vision of a faith community. We give some samples of such prayers indicating in each case their context within the group that uses them. As it is common to all Christians, we do not treat of the *Our Father*, which was considered in another context in chapter five. From thousands of prayers available in anthologies, we select a few, but seek to indicate how their meaning can be grasped. Since they are well known and immediately assessable, we do not consider prayers in the Judaeo-Christian scriptures. There are also other prayers in other chapters of this volume.

Catholic prayers: The *Hail Mary* and Rosary

A feature of Roman Catholicism and of Eastern Christian Churches like the Orthodox, is the important role for Blessed Mary the Mother of God. This tradition is very old; the most ancient prayer, *Sub tuum* (Latin opening words, 'under your') to Mary is from the third century:

> We fly to your patronage O holy Mother of God. Despise not our prayers in our necessities, but ever deliver us from all danger, O glorious and Blessed Virgin Mary.

Thousands of prayers followed in this tradition.

One of the most popular prayers in the Roman tradition is the *Hail Mary* (*Ave Maria*). The first part is from Luke's gospel: 'Hail Mary full of grace, the Lord is with you', (1:28). The words 'full of grace' are from the ancient Latin translation of the New Testament called the Vulgate; 'Rejoice, you who have received and are receiving favour' is a trifle nearer the Greek. The next phrase 'Blessed are you among women', is from Elizabeth's greeting (1:42). Hebrew does not have a superlative, so the original idea may be 'you are the most blessed of all.' The next words again come from Elizabeth, 'blessed is the fruit of your womb' (1:42). The idiom here is Hebrew; it means, of course, 'your child is blessed' (see idiom also in Luke 11:27). These phrases are found in prayers from the fifth century. By the eleventh century they are together in offices, or devotions, in honour of Our Lady. The name 'Jesus' and 'Amen' were added from about the fourteenth century. Phrases of the second part, 'Holy Mary Mother of God pray for us now and at the hour of our death', appear from the eleventh century, but the prayer became invariable only with Pope St Pius V in 1568.

From the eleventh century too it was customary to honour Mary with 150 greetings beginning with the word *Ave*, the number being that of the psalms that monks said. In time reflections were added to the recitation of the *Ave*. In time these were simplified to the first part of the *Hail* Mary. The list of reflections was reduced also to fifteen. So by the fifteenth century we have fifteen reflections each lasting the space of ten *Aves*. Beads or knotted rope for counting emerged in the twelfth century. By the late fifteenth century the Rosary (from German *Rosenkranz*, a rose garden), was taking present shape. The *Our Father* was added a century later, then the *Gloria* and the *Apostles Creed* in the seventeenth century. In its modern form the Rosary was approved in 1569 by the same pope, Pius V. It remained unchanged in the three sets of mysteries until recent times. There are five considerations about the infancy of Jesus (Joyful Mysteries: Annunciation, Visitation to Elizabeth, Nativity, Presentation of Jesus in the Temple, the Finding of Jesus after he had been lost three days); five about the Passion of the Lord (Sorrowful Mysteries: Agony in the Garden, Scourging, Crowning with Thorns, Way of the Cross, Crucifixion); and five about his triumph (Glorious Mysteries: Resurrection, Ascension, Pentecost, Assumption of Mary and her Coronation). The Rosary became very popular among Catholics. Many popes have encouraged it. In recent years Pope John Paul II wrote an important letter on the Rosary, explaining its value and giving advice on how it might best be said.[2] In it he added a fourth set of mysteries to cover the time between the Finding of Jesus at the age of twelve and the Agony in the Garden. These he called 'Mysteries of Light' (Baptism of the Lord, the Wedding at Cana, Conversion and the Preaching of the Kingdom, the Transfiguration, the Last Supper).

A note about saints
In many religions there is profound respect for the memory of holy persons. People look to their example. They may even be seen as living commentaries on the sacred texts of a faith community. Being associated with a culture, they help to show a particular people how to live in a profoundly religious way.[3] In general one can make a sharp distinction between the traditions of the Roman Catholic and Orthodox Churches and almost all other believers. These two Churches actively encourage invocation of saints: people pray to them, so that they in turn may intercede, adding their holy prayers to God for the petitioner. In the Roman Catholic and Orthodox Churches Mary the Mother of the Lord is held in special veneration.

Anglican prayer tradition
Anglicanism has a rich prayer tradition. To grasp it fully we should keep in mind some features of Anglicanism. Its sources for belief are scripture, tradition and reason. Under tradition are included the major Councils of the Church and the great

Church Fathers of the East and West. A second feature of Anglicanism is its self-conscious attempt to be a *via media*, that is, a middle way between the two perceived extremes of Rome and Geneva, called the Elizabethan Settlement. At various times influences from Rome (Catholicism) and Geneva (Calvinism) have appeared. In general, one could say that Anglicanism has a quasi-horror of exaggeration. A third feature has been called the 'Anglican ethos'. The Anglican author W. Taylor Stevenson notes that ethos here is rather intractable because it consists of underlying assumptions and feelings, and because they are underlying, they go unchallenged and thereby dominate the group. He goes on to say that an ethos is a 'habit of the mind', but more importantly is constituted by 'habits of the heart' – a way of being in the world. He indicates two aspects of the English ethos: 'First, there is the assumption that consensus, comprehensiveness and contract is the normative way of establishing and maintaining the order of society... second, there is in the English ethos a certain pragmatism and lack of speculative interest in the approach to human affairs.'[4] These characteristics can be found in the Anglican prayer tradition.

Anglicanism takes very seriously the adage quoted above, *lex orandi, lex credendi*. In fact one can say that its main liturgical text, *The Book of Common Prayer* (BCP) expresses the core of the community's faith. An Anglican scholar, L. Weil notes:

> In no other Christian tradition does the authorized liturgy take on so great a significance. The Prayer Book is first of all the basis for corporate worship... In addition to this essential role, and as a kind of natural overflow from it, the Prayer book is also a formative element in the private prayer of Anglicans. Even in solitude, the use of the collects or psalms, or the texts of the various rites, link the individual at prayer with the

common prayer of the larger fellowship. Again the
Prayer Book is also turned to as a source for the teaching
of the Church. Anglicanism gives forceful expression to
the ancient adage, *Lex orandi, legem statuat credendi*, 'the
law of prayer establishes the law of faith'.[5]

The translation here of the Latin aphorism, or tag, at the end
is one of several found among scholars. The paragraph gives
some idea of the importance of the Church of England BCP;
it is an expression of the insistence of the primacy of liturgy in
the life of the Church. Its text is largely the work of the
Archbishop of Canterbury, Thomas Cranmer (1489-1553). He
consciously sought the middle way mentioned earlier. He
produced a great masterpiece of the English language as well
as a book that has given unity to a worldwide communion of
Churches.

We can take two examples from the English BCP. The first
is the collect (from Latin *colligere*, to gather) for purity at the
opening of the Communion service; the word 'collect' in
liturgical language originally meant a prayer of one sentence
that 'gathers up' and expresses a petition on behalf of all the
people:

> Almighty God, unto whom all hearts be open, all desires
> known, and from whom no secrets are hid: Cleanse the
> thoughts of our hearts by the inspiration of thy Holy
> Spirit, that we may perfectly love thee, and worthily
> magnify thy holy Name; through Christ our Lord.
> Amen.

The second is the collect for help against all perils, taken from
Evening Prayer:

> Lighten our darkness, we beseech thee, O Lord; and by
> thy great mercy defend us from all perils and dangers of

this night; for the love of thy only Son, our Saviour, Jesus Christ. Amen.

The great Methodist scholar G. Wainwright comments on these prayers:

> Notice how the total effect is achieved through a variety of things such as rhythm, parallelism, balance, word pairs, contrasts, biblical echoes, archetypal ideas, and the discreet use of affective language. Memorable prayers in the fixed parts of the liturgy allow the worshippers to be disencumbered from book and relish the spoken word.[6]

The prayers have to be read aloud slowly to catch something of their aesthetic perfection.

There is of course a problem with the BCP. Its glorious language, and that of the *King James Bible* (Authorised Version), for all its beauty is now archaic. There have been many attempts to revise the BCP in various Churches of the Anglican Communion; for several years the Church of Ireland worked on a further revision. In the prayers quoted above from the English BCP there are only slight modifications to modernise the speech.

> Almighty God, to whom all hearts are open, all desires known, and from whom no secrets are hidden: Cleanse the thoughts of our hearts by the inspiration of your Holy Spirit, that we may perfectly love thee, and worthily magnify your holy Name; through Christ our Lord. Amen.

And,

> Lighten our darkness, O Lord, we pray; and in your great mercy defend us from all perils and dangers of this

night; for the love of thy only Son, our Saviour, Jesus Christ. Amen.[7]

Reactions to changes vary. Some people much prefer the older texts and find the modern revisions harsh and too prosaic; others find the older texts a hindrance to genuine personal prayer. The mixed reception of vernacular liturgy in the Roman Catholic Church gives an idea of how the matter of language can arouse very strong feelings.

Apart from the worship of the sacraments there is a very strong tradition in Anglicanism of Morning and Evening prayer. It has been said that the most successful of all the Reformation offices was the Anglican one. Clergy are expected to say these two offices and many laity do so too, or use prayer forms based on the Morning or Evening Prayer of the BCP.[8] The structure is somewhat simpler than the Roman Catholic *Liturgy of the Hours*; the elements of psalms, hymns, scripture and prayers are common. The new Church of Ireland BCP also has a collection of prayers for various occasions.[9]

Another source for Anglican prayer is the Metaphysical poets such as John Donne (1571/2-1631), George Herbert (1593-1633), Thomas Traherne (*c.* 1637-1674) – all clergymen – and Henry Vaughan (1622-1695). Their poems in differing styles often revolve around the fact of human sin and divine love. We can take as an example one of the 'Holy Sonnets' of John Donne, found also in the Roman Catholic *Liturgy of the Hours*:

> Batter my heart, three-personed God, for you
> As yet but knock, breathe, shine, and seek to mend;
> That I may rise and stand, o'erthrow me and bend
> Your force to break, blow, burn and make me new.
> I, like an usurped town to another due,
> Labour to admit you, but O, to no end.
> Reason, your viceroy within me, me should defend,
> But is captivated and proves weak or untrue.

Yet dearly I love you and would be loved fain,
But am betrothed to your enemy.
Divorce me, untie me, or break that knot again,
Take me to you, imprison me, for I,
Except you enthral me, never shall be free,
Nor ever chaste unless you ravish me.

Here the story of salvation is depicted as the tug between sin and God's love, described under the central image of a castle under a tyrant, sin.

Methodist prayer tradition

Methodism goes back to John Wesley (1703-1791). As an undergraduate in Oxford he was a member of a group, called 'the Holy Club', which took faith and practice in the Church of England with great seriousness. Though its exact origins are disputed, 'Methodism' became an appellation for methodical pursuit of Christian holiness. In time John Wesley took to itinerant preaching around Britain. His sermons were extremely powerful and led to a profound revival in Christian practice, especially among poorer people in the new Industrial Revolution. He began his English outdoor preaching among mineworkers. He is alleged to have travelled 200,000 miles, mostly on horseback and to have preached 40,000 sermons. In a complex history, which need not concern us here, his followers broke with (or were frozen out of?) the Church of England and became an autonomous Church after Wesley's death.

The prayer tradition of Methodism reflects John Wesley and his brother Charles. John experienced two major conversions, which opened him up to the experiential dimension of faith. His preaching was not novel in content, but was original in its focus and power. He preached a scriptural doctrine with a Protestant flavour, emphasising salvation by faith, new birth, and the work of the Holy Spirit. He constantly spoke of God's universal love, the power of grace to counter human depravity, and an assurance given by the Spirit that people are children of God (see Rom 8:16). Methodist piety has a strong biblical clarity as well as appeal to experience. It is found not so much in prayers as in the hymns, which John and especially his brother Charles wrote. These have indelibly characterised the Methodist soul. An example from the hymns of Charles, 'The Holy Spirit', will show their main features: solid theology, awareness of human sin and grace, warmth and clarity.

> O you who comes from above
> The pure celestial fire to impart,
> Kindle a flame of sacred love
> On the mean altar of my heart.
>
> There let it be for thy glory burn
> With inextinguishable blaze,
> And trembling to its source return
> In humble prayer, and fervent praise.
>
> Jesus, confirm my heart's desire
> To work, and speak, and think for thee;
> Still let me guard the holy fire
> And still stir up thy gift in me.
>
> Ready for all thy perfect will,
> My acts of faith and love repeat,
> Til death thy endless mercies seal
> And make my sacrifice complete.[10]

Celtic prayer tradition

There has been in recent decades enormous interest in Celtic spirituality. Not all of it is sufficiently scholarly or accurate; people can seek a basis for New Age spiritualities in what they claim to find in the Celtic tradition. Though there are many similarities among Celtic countries, especially between Scotland and Ireland, we concentrate on the Irish dimension. There are two main sources for Celtic religion: firstly monuments and archaeological remains; secondly, literature which begins to appear in the second half of the sixth century. Where there is no contemporary literature the former is open to very diverse interpretations, even with the help of an oral tradition written down much later.

In Celtic religion there is a great accent on fertility, with the sun and the wheel being important symbols. The myths associated with place-names shows that primitive Celtic spirituality was very much centred on nature: mountaintops, clearings, rivers, springs, and sacred trees. There are also accounts of animal imagery: bulls (*Táin Bó Cuailnge*), ravens, stags, salmon, serpents, boars, horses, and birds. Reflecting on these traditions there would come in time a deep sense of the omnipresence of the divine, which is seen as immanent in the created order.

When we come to Celtic prayer we find that it reflects the vivid sense of God who is close at hand. The Celtic scholar, Douglas Hyde (first *Uachtarán* (President) of Ireland) wrote: 'The Gaelic race see the hand of God in every place, in every time and in every thing... They have this sense of being embraced on all sides by God.'[11] The prayers collected in Ireland by Hyde, and by A. Carmichael in Scotland, are an oral tradition which is essentially a lay spirituality; praying is not necessarily associated with going to church.[12] The hymn ascribed to St Patrick, 'Christ be before me', reflects this aspect of prayer.

From the many collections of Irish prayers we take a few from the fine volume of the late Diarmuid Ó Laoghaire.[13] The first is during work; the second is on its completion:

> *A Íosa ionúin, toirbhrim mé féin duit idir anam agus corp mar aon leis an obair seo.*

A Íosa a mhilse mo chroí, tabhair grá lasúin dom ort.

A Íosa mo dhóigh is mo shólás, tabhair dom do thoil a dhéanamh

A Mhuire a Mháthair na ngrás, neartaigh agus cuidigh liom.

Dear Jesus, I give myself to you, body and soul, along with this work.

Jesus delight of my heart, give me a warm love for you.

Jesus my hope and my salvation, grant me to do your will.

Mary, Mother of grace, strengthen and help me.

Beannacht Dé le hanamann' na marbh, is go bhfága Dia mór ár saol is ár sláinte again, agus go gcuire Dia rath ar ár saothar is ar shaothar na gCríostaithe.

God's blessing on the souls of the dead. May almighty God leave us life and health, and may God bless our work and the work of all Christians.[14]

Some features of Irish prayer already appear. There is humanity and warmth about such prayers. They have a close sense of God's presence. The Irish devotion or concern for the souls of the departed appears, as well as a deep devotion to Mary.[15] This last is found in a common saying: *Tá Dia láidir agus tá Máthair mhaith aige* (God is strong and he has a good Mother).[16] Another feature of Celtic prayer is the strong sense of the Communion of Saints – the fellowship between those in heaven and those on earth, e.g. a prayer against drowning:

Mary and her Son,
Patrick with his staff,
Martin with his mantle
Brighid with her hood
Michael with his shield,

And God before them all
With his strong right arm. Amen.[17]

Along with prayers for all occasions, there are also blessings and
short prayers for many situations; Ó Laoghaire gives more than
four hundred. Some examples:

> [A general blessing] *Go bhféacha Dia orainn agus Muire
> Mháthair*
> May God look upon us, and Mother Mary.
> *Toil Dé go ndéantar*
> God's will be done.
> [Thanksgiving for a drink] *Go dtuga Dia deoch as tobar na
> ngrást duit*
> May God give you a drink from the well of grace.
> [On hearing that a person has done wrong]
> *Nár agraí Dia air é* and *Nár thóga Dia air é*
> May God not hold it against him.
> [On hearing bad news] *Dia idir sinn agus an anachain*
> God between us and all harm.[18]

This Celtic tradition of prayer would seem to have much to
teach Christians who wish to avoid what Vatican II called 'one of
the graves errors of our time', namely 'the dichotomy between
the faith which may profess and their day-to-day conduct.'[19]

Jewish Prayer tradition

A core part of the Jewish prayer tradition will already be familiar
to Christians in the Psalms of the Bible. There are also many
devotional books and prayers used frequently, or daily, by devout
Jews such as grace at meals. In the following prayer used in the
daily service, one can easily pick up biblical echoes.

> Cause us, our Father, to lie down in peace, and to rise
> again to enjoy life. Spread over us the covering of Your

peace, guide us with Your good counsel and save us for the sake of Your name. Be a shield about us, turning away every enemy, disease, violence, hunger and sorrow. Shelter us in the shadow of Your wings, for You are a God who guards and protects us, a ruler of mercy and compassion. Guard us when we go out and when we come in, to enjoy life and peace, both now and forever, and spread over us the shelter of Your peace. Blessed are You Lord, who spreads the shelter of peace over us, over his people Israel, and over all the world.[20]

The God of Jewish prayer is transcendent and absolute, but is close to his people in mercy.

Islamic prayer

We have already considered the *Salat* or Muslim daily prayer in an earlier chapter. There is, however, a further rich tradition of personal piety in Islam: the liturgical is matched with the practice of *du'â*, or calling upon God. There are many prayers in the Qur'an. In an earlier chapter we have alluded to the ninety-nine 'most beautiful names' of God. God has to be named so that people may call upon him. In such prayer theology and worship are united. *Du'â* is closely akin to *dhikr*, a rich word which has connotations of both remembering and mentioning. The Muslim recalls the presence of God in response to being addressed by God. Constant themes are the greatness of Allah, peace, forgiveness and protection from spiritual and temporal ills, seeking refuge in Him and desiring to see His face. We take a prayer from Zain al'Abidin, great-grandson of the Prophet Muhammad:

O my God, only Your kindness and compassion can restore my brokenness. My poverty nothing can enrich but Your gentleness and goodness. Only grace from You can calm my agitation. My frailty Your power alone can strengthen. My longings nothing but Your bounty will ever satisfy. My destitution will be made good by Your wealth alone. My need of You none other can fulfil. Only Your mercy can gladden my distress. My sorrow of heart only Your compassion will relieve. My thirst will not be slaked unless You reach to me, nor my fearing soul be set at rest except I find You. Only the sight of Your countenance of grace can meet my deepest yearning. It is only in drawing near to You that rest is truly mine... O my God, do mercy to Your unworthy servant, whose word is faint, whose deed is scant. In Your rich forbearance do well to him. Shelter him under Your shade, You who are the Lord of all the merciful, kingly, glorious and merciful.[21]

Finally, we might add a short Muslim prayer, which illustrates the strong faith in eternal life:

O Lord, may the end of my life be the best of it; may my closing acts be my best acts, and may the best of my days be the day when I shall meet Thee.[22]

Conclusion

One of the results of examining other prayer traditions should surely be greater respect for other peoples, and in Ireland for the many refugees and immigrants from Islamic cultures. The political and military activities of the State of Israel and of the followers of Muhammad grab the headlines. But more important for the future of our world is the rich tradition of holiness in the great Abrahamic religions. These prayers that we have considered show us that these religions, as well as Christianity, are all dealing with flawed human beings whose only hope of healing lies in God's help. An awareness of the spiritual heritage of other Christians can help us to have a truer picture of them than the one presented in the Northern 'marching season'. Roman Catholics will want to read this section along with the earlier chapter on sacraments, which are the highest expression of their prayer and worship.

Notes

1.   Congregation for Divine Worship and the Discipline of the Sacraments, *Directory on Popular Piety and the Liturgy: Principles and Guidelines* (London: St Pauls Publishing, 2002), n. 9, p.21. The whole text is available on the Vatican Site: see *www.vatican.va*, then site map, then Divine Worship, Congregation, then 2002 documents.

2.   Apostolic Letter, *Rosarium Virginis Mariae* (2002) available on Vatican website.

3.   On saints see: D. Attwater, *Penguin Dictionary of Saints* (London: Penguin Books, 1995); J.N.D. Kelly, *The Oxford Dictionary of Saints* (Oxford: University Press, 1988).

4.   W. Taylor Stevenson, 'Lex Orandi – Lex Credendi' in *The Study of Anglicanism*. Ed. S. Sykes and J. Booty (London: SPCK /Philadelphia: Fortress, 1988) pp. 174-185 at 177.

5.   L. Weil, 'The Gospel in Anglicanism' in *The Study of Anglicanism*, pp. 51-76 at 55.

6.   G. Wainwright, 'The Language of Worship' in *The Study of Liturgy*. Ed. C. Jones, G. Wainwright and E. Yarnold (London: SPCK, 1978 with frequent reprints), pp. 465-473 at 473.

7.   *The Book of Common Prayer according to the use of the Church of Ireland* (Dublin: Columba, 2004) pp. 201, 115.

8.   For example, B. Mayne, *As We Believe So Do We Pray: A Book of Daily Prayer* (Dublin: Columba, 2004).

9.   Irish BCP, pp. 145-153

10. G. Appleton, ed., *The Oxford Book of Prayer* (Oxford: University Press, paperback, 1968, 2002), n. 683, p. 211.

11. Cited E. de Waal, *The Celtic Way of Prayer* (New York/London: Doubleday, 1995), p. 70.

12. De Waal, *Celtic Way*, p. 72.

13. D. Ó Laoghaire, ed. *Ár bPaidreacha Dúchais: Cnuasach de Paidreachta agus de Bhannachtai ár Sinsear* (Dublin: Foilseacháin Ábhair Spioradálta, 1982); see also *Saltai: Urnaithe Dúchais. Prayers from the Irish Tradition*. Ed. P. Ó Fiannachta, trans. D. Forristal (Dublin:

Columba, 1988); R. MacCróaigh, tr. *Prayers of the Gael: A Translation of Charlotte Dease, Paidreachta na nDaoine* (London: Sands/St Louis: Herder, 1914).

14. Ó Laoghaire, *Ár bPaidreacha Dúchais*, pp. 60-61; also *Saltair*, pp. 14-17.

15. See P. O'Dwyer, *Mary: A History of Devotion in Ireland* (Dublin: Four Courts, 1988); D. Ó Laoghaire, 'Celtic Prayer' in P. Clancy, ed., *Celtic Threads: Exploring the Wisdom of Our Heritage* (Dublin: Veritas, 1999), pp. 71089 at 79.

16. Ó Laoghaire, *Ár bPaidreacha*, p. 179.

17. R. MacCrócaigh, *Prayers of the Gael*, p. 41.

18. Ó Laoghaire, *Ár bPaidreacha*, pp. 246, 250

19. Vatican II: *Constitution on the Church in the Modern World* GS 43,

20. Appleton, *Oxford Book* n. 837, p. 275.

21. Appleton, *Oxford Book*, pp. 334-335.

22. Appleton, *Oxford Book*, p. 344.

Select Bibliography

G. Appleton, ed., *The Oxford Book of Prayer* (Oxford: University Press, paperback, 1968, 2002). A rich book of over a thousand prayers from more than a dozen faiths.

Congregation for Divine Worship and the Discipline of the Sacraments, *Directory on Popular Piety and the Liturgy: Principles and Guidelines* (London: St Pauls Publishing, 2002). The whole text is available on the Vatican Site: see www.vatican.va then site map, then Divine Worship, Congregation, then 2002. The well-produced index and contents will give information on many of the topics, which arise in the Syllabus G, 'Worship, Prayer and Ritual.'

P. Ó Fiannachta, ed., *Saltai: Urnaithe Dúchais. Prayers from the Irish Tradition*. Trans. D.Forristal (Dublin: Columba, 1988).

D. Ó Laoghaire, ed., *Ár bPaidreacha Dúchais: Cnuasach de Paidreachta agus de Bhannachtaí ár Sinsear* (Dublin: Foilseacháin Ábhair Spioradálta, 1982).

Part Three

MEDITATION AND CONTEMPLATION

8

Meditation

With meditation we are again faced with problems of meaning. It may seem tiresome to be establishing meaning in each section, but in spirituality there is no fixed language and we have to determine meaning from a general context and from the specific use that is found in a particular author. There are very particular difficulties with meditation because of the enormous range of meanings and the vastly different contexts in which it is used. As we have already noted, a secular dictionary does not provide much help, but for what it is worth we give the following:

> **Meditate**, to consider thoughtfully (with *on* or *upon*): to engage in contemplation, especially religious *v.t.* to consider deeply, reflect upon, to revolve in the mind, to intend. [The derivation is given as Latin *meditari*, probably cognate with *mederi*, to heal.][1]

The great religious traditions all stress the importance of a quiet prayer that ponders. But meditation is also of interest to people who are not concerned with its religious aspects, but who are seeking psychological or physical health, relaxation and integrity in a world of stress. We can see meditation as an example of the need for reflection considered in an earlier chapter.

In this chapter we shall seek some consistency in language, but the reader needs to be aware of the range of meanings found in works on prayer and spirituality. Furthermore it seems clear that to address fully the demands of the syllabus (see 'Christian meditation as an experience of encounter') we need to take account of what the *Catechism* says about both meditation and contemplative prayer.

The Judaeo-Christian tradition

Already in the Old Testament there is an emphasis on pondering, thinking about the Lord's law. The just 'meditate on the law of God day and night' (Ps 1:2). The longest of the psalms, and a great favourite of the early Irish monks, is a celebration of God's ways mulled over by the faithful Jew; it uses many synonyms all with the general sense of the Law as God's will (see Ps 119:1-176). Those who retire to think about God's ways are seen as wise, like Joseph in the Old Testament (see Gen 37:37:11; Wis 12:22; Sir 14:20; 39:7); Mary in the New Testament ponders in her heart (see Luke 2:19.51).

In the Christian tradition meditation is religious: it focuses on God or on the relation of the person with the divine. An outline of the Catholic tradition on meditation can be found in the *Catechism*:

> Meditation is above all a quest. The mind seeks to understand the why and how of the Christian life, in order to adhere and respond to what the Lord is asking. The required attentiveness is difficult to sustain. We are usually helped by books, and Christians do not want for them: the Sacred Scriptures, particularly the Gospels, holy icons, liturgical texts of the day or season, writings of the spiritual fathers, works of spirituality, the great book of creation, and that of history, the page on which the 'today' of God is written. (2705)

This meditation is active; it involves the mind, the imagination. It often involves reflection on a sacred text. There is in meditation a kind of education. It is not that we meditate to learn more, but rather to appropriate more, to enter into and grasp the inner meaning of the text. The aim is not purely intellectual. Meditation seeks to integrate belief and life. Again the *Catechism*:

> To meditate on what we read helps us to make it our own by confronting it with ourselves. Here, another book is opened: the book of life. We pass from thoughts to reality. To the extent that we are humble and faithful, we discover in meditation the movements that stir the heart and we are able to discern them. It is a question of acting truthfully in order to come into the light: 'Lord, what do you want me to do?' (2706).

Such meditation is not aimed at self-improvement, but seeks conformity with God's plan. The *Catechism* again notes 'there are as many and varied methods of meditation as there are spiritual masters. Christians owe it to themselves to develop the desire to meditate regularly, lest they come to resemble the three first kinds of soil in the parable of the sower.' The reference here is to the possibility that the word of God may not take root in people's lives (see Mark 4:4-7.15-19).

There are indeed many methods of Christian meditation. The *Catechism* notes that 'a method is only a guide; the important thing is to advance, with the Holy Spirit, along the one way of prayer: Christ Jesus' (2707). These methods show how people are to engage 'thought, imagination, emotion, and desire. This mobilization of faculties is necessary in order to deepen our convictions of faith, prompt the conversion of our heart, and strengthen our will to follow Christ.' How the imagination and the senses are to be used will vary according to different methods.

Ignatian meditation

The method found in the *Spiritual Exercises* of St Ignatius of
Loyola (d. 1556) shows the value of fully engaging oneself.
Meditation for Ignatius is set in a religious context. It is always
to be preceded by a prayer that what follows will be to the
praise of God.[2] The next step is to imagine the scene, the
situation that is the topic of the meditation; one next asks for
the grace needed. Then the meditation unfolds. It is always
concluded by what Ignatius calls a 'colloquy', that is, a
conversation with God. As one speaks to a friend or to a master,
'now asking for a favour, now blaming oneself for some
misdeed, now making known one's concerns or seeking
advice'.[3] The contemplation on the Nativity of the Lord gives
some sense of this active meditation:

> **Prayer.** The usual Preparatory Prayer.
>
> **First Prelude.** The first Prelude is the narrative and it
> will be here how Our Lady went forth from Nazareth,
> about nine months with child, as can be piously
> meditated, seated on an ass, and accompanied by Joseph
> and a maid, taking an ox, to go to Bethlehem to pay the
> tribute which Caesar imposed on all those lands.
>
> **Second Prelude.** The second, a composition, seeing the
> place. It will be here to see with the sight of the
> imagination the road from Nazareth to Bethlehem;
> considering the length and the breadth, and whether
> such road is level or through valleys or over hills; likewise
> looking at the place or cave of the Nativity, how large,
> how small, how low, how high, and how it was prepared.
>
> **Third Prelude.** This is to ask for what I desire. Here it
> will be to ask for an intimate knowledge of our Lord,
> who has become man for me, that I may love him more
> and follow him more closely.
>
> **First Point.** The first point is to see the persons; that is,
> to see Our Lady and Joseph and the maid, and, after His

Birth, the Child Jesus, I making myself a poor creature and a wretch of an unworthy slave, looking at them and serving them in their needs, with all possible respect and reverence, as if I found myself present; and then to reflect on myself in order to draw some profit.

Second Point. The second, to look, mark and contemplate what they are saying, and, reflecting on myself, to draw some profit.

Third Point. The third, to look and consider what they are doing, as going a journey and labouring, that the Lord may be born in the greatest poverty; and as a termination of so many labours – of hunger, of thirst, of heat and of cold, of injuries and affronts – that He may die on the Cross; and all this for me: then reflecting, to draw some spiritual profit.

Colloquy. I will finish with a Colloquy as in the preceding Contemplation, and with an Our Father.[4]

Some people may think that this method of meditation is too highly structured. However, it has a lot of flexibility and allows a person to delay at one point whilst moving more quickly over others. Its advantage as a method is that it encourages the use of imagination, reasoning, desire, as well as wide-ranging reflection. The specifics given above are only indications of how a person might meditate on Bethlehem.

Lectio divina

Throughout the centuries Christians meditated on the scriptures. It is easy however to read a passage then wander into all kinds of thoughts that may have nothing to do with meditation. The text of Luke 12:28 about the grass of the field could easily move by association of ideas to farming, football fields, or marijuana. The Christian tradition of lectio divina (sacred reading) provides a structure and a focus for meditation on the scriptures. It originated in the monasteries and in the

Middle Ages was widespread among the friars also. The early practice consisted of reading the text aloud – not all monks were literate, and they did not have copies of the bible available to each one. *Lectio divina* can take place in groups or individually.

There are four Latin words used about the method to describe each of its phases. These, however, are what linguistics calls 'false friends', that is, the similar or derived English word does not give an accurate translation.

The first stage is **reading** (*lectio*). The text is carefully read. One asks what is going on? Who is there? What are they saying? and so on. The question here is what does the text mean. Very often it will be the verbs that will alert one to the text.

The second stage is **reflection** (*meditatio*). Here one actively reflects on the text asking how it applies to life, what its significance is at this time, what are its practical implications. The ancient monks often spoke of this phase as 'ruminating' like an animal chewing the cud, seeking to draw full nourishment from what it has eaten. The key question here can be expressed as: what does the text mean to me?

The third stage is **response** (*oratio*). Here one speaks to God in the light of what one has thought about the text. This is similar to the Ignatian colloquy: one addresses God as a friend about whatever is significant in one's life, especially in the light of the previous stages.

The fourth stage is **resting** (*contemplatio*). One stays silently with the text, allowing oneself to be drawn by it. Here one is less active; one may just have one thought or idea that holds one's attention. One might think of it as a backward glance at a scene that one is leaving, or even plucking a flower to take with one.

Since the four stages are prayer, and all are a method of meditation, one can see how the Latin words might mislead. The English four R's are preferable, but the Latin words need to be understood, since they are commonly found.

Again as in the case of Ignatian prayer, a person may pose the objection that the method is too structured. It too is flexible, and it has the advantage of providing a framework within which there can be great spontaneity in prayer.

Development

The *Catechism of the Catholic Church* observes that one should not remain at meditation but should move on to deeper love of God. But its language in the English translation is somewhat unhelpful. It distinguishes three expressions of prayer: vocal prayer (2700-2704), meditation (2705-2708) and contemplative prayer (2709-2719). We should remember that the *Catechism* was initially written in French, and the original gave three expressions of prayer: *la prière vocale, la méditation* and *l'oraison*. What the English version calls contemplative prayer and the French *oraison* is explained explicitly using St Teresa of Avila's definition of what she calls 'mental prayer'. The English text even gives us the Spanish words:

> What is contemplative prayer? St Teresa answers, 'Contemplative prayer [*oración mental*] in my opinion is nothing else than a close sharing between friends; it means taking time frequently to be alone with him who we know loves us.' (2709)

Some people consider this to be the heart of Christian meditation. Others will use the word 'contemplation' for a higher form of meditation in which prayer becomes more simple, with less activity of the intellect and imagination. There is a further distinction between various levels of contemplation: some may be cultivated by using certain forms and structures; a higher form is pure gift from God and cannot be acquired by human effort alone. This second level belongs more to an account of mysticism.

In summary form the *Catechism* distinguishes the three kinds of prayer.

1. Vocal prayer, founded on the union of body and soul in human nature, associates the body with the interior prayer of the heart, following Christ's example of praying to his Father and teaching the *Our Father* to his disciples.

2. Meditation is a prayerful quest engaging thought, imagination, emotion, and desire. Its goal is to make our own in faith the subject considered, by confronting it with the reality of our own life.

3. Contemplative prayer is the simple expression of the mystery of prayer. It is a gaze of faith fixed on Jesus, an attentiveness to the Word of God, a silent love. It achieves real union with the prayer of Christ to the extent that it makes us share in his mystery. (2722-2724)

Further on contemplative prayer the *Catechism* notes:

> Contemplative prayer is the prayer of the child of God, of the forgiven sinner who agrees to welcome the love by which he is loved and who wants to respond to it by loving even more. But he knows that the love he is returning is poured out by the Spirit in his heart, for everything is grace from God. Contemplative prayer is the poor and humble surrender to the loving will of the Father in ever-deeper union with his beloved Son.
>
> Contemplative prayer is the simplest expression of the mystery of prayer. It is a gift, a grace; it can be accepted only in humility and poverty. Contemplative prayer is a covenant relationship established by God within our hearts. Contemplative prayer is a communion in which

the Holy Trinity conforms man, the image of God, 'to his likeness.'

Contemplative prayer is also the pre-eminently intense time of prayer. In it the Father strengthens our inner being with power through his Spirit 'that Christ may dwell in [our] hearts through faith' and we may be 'grounded in love.'

Contemplation is a gaze of faith, fixed on Jesus. 'I look at him and he looks at me': This is what a certain peasant of Ars in the time of its holy Curé [St John Vianney, d. 1859] used to say while praying before the tabernacle. This focus on Jesus is a renunciation of self. His gaze purifies our heart; the light of the countenance of Jesus illumines the eyes of our heart and teaches us to see everything in the light of his truth and his compassion for all men. Contemplation also turns its gaze on the mysteries of the life of Christ. Thus it learns the 'interior knowledge of our Lord,' the more to love him and follow him. (2712-2715)

This form of prayer involves some simplification. It can come after people have been meditating some time.

Praying with a mantra

In secular use one finds the word 'mantra' used as meaning something that a person, or an advertisement, keeps repeating. But the word is originally religious; it comes from Sanskrit and means a sacred word. In Asian religions one finds a tradition of repeating a sacred word of text that is seen as a word of power. It has the effect of focusing the attention beyond imagination and thought and so brings the person into the reality of the divine sphere. The Benedictine monk, John Main (1926-1982)[5], learned this tradition from an Indian teacher and he adopted it to Christian prayer. There is some evidence of a mantra type prayer in the Christian tradition, e.g. in the fourteenth-century spiritual classic *The Cloud of Unknowing* (ch. 7). Main suggests a Christian word like *Maranatha* (see 1 Cor 16:22 where it means either 'the Lord is coming – *maran atha*' or 'Lord come! – *marana tha*').

John Main recommends repeating the mantra for about twenty to thirty minutes both morning and evening. One is to keep saying the word quietly, concentrating only on it until we are silent. He adds that to decide to stop saying the word is to begin thinking, and one should return to the mantra, for its purifying emptiness. In his lifetime many meditation groups have sprung up where people sometimes together and then alone engage in meditation.

In the Christian East there is found the 'Jesus Prayer' that is quietly recited over and over, often with the help of beads. It has many forms, a common one being 'Lord Jesus Christ, Son of God, have mercy on me a sinner.' It is not strictly speaking a mantra, as there is quite explicit thinking of Jesus and reaching out towards him during its recitation.

Centering Prayer

Rather similar to the John Main method of meditation is centering prayer, popularised by a Cistercian, Thomas Keating.[6] This arises out of the *lectio divina* method, but is more focused on its fourth stage, contemplation, which we have called 'resting'. A key insight is that God dwells within us. This is also found in St Teresa of Avila, who counselled going within, to listen, to speak and to gaze. We go within not to find ourselves, but to find God; in the process, we do of course find our deepest self. Keating recommends five states:[7]

1. Choose a sacred word as a symbol of your intention to open and yield to God's presence and action within you.
2. Sitting comfortably, and with eyes closed introduce the sacred word as the symbol of your consent to God's presence and action within.

3. When you become aware of thoughts, return ever so gently to the sacred word. It is a matter of remaining centered on it.
4. The term 'thoughts' includes any perceptions: ideas, feelings, images, memories... There are to be no expectations in this prayer.
5. Some silence with eyes closed to allow the psyche to adjust to the world to which you are returning.

A name very much associated with Main and Keating is Basil Pennington, who has written extensively on centering prayer.[8] Keating observes,

> Centering prayer is not an end in itself but a beginning. It is not done for the sake of enjoying spiritual consolation but for the sake of its positive fruits in one's life: charity, joy, peace, self-knowledge, compassion, inner freedom, humility.[9]

The context of centering prayer is important as well as its openness to spiritual growth.[10]

Practical issues

Meditation has great values. But it is not easy. The great teachers of meditation will all insist that progress in the spiritual journey needs consistent efforts. If one finds meditation helpful, then a phase of stress like approaching examinations is not a time to stop meditation to save time for study, but rather it will give more benefits, such as allowing relaxation, placing the examinations into perspective, invoking God's help, being comforted by an awareness of God's presence and care. In St Teresa's definition of prayer earlier in this chapter, we should notice the word 'frequently' about contemplative prayer; a relationship of love or friendship cannot be effectively cultivated by stops and starts.

In all forms of meditation we encounter problems with our bodies and with our thoughts. Experience teaches that lounging on an armchair will not assist meditation, or other serious thinking. We will usually do better by physically bringing our bodies into some form of relaxed unity. Such methods will involve keeping our legs or feet together, our hands loosely joined or stress-free, our spine straight, and perhaps our eyes closed. Calm breathing too is help. Inside of ourselves we have greater problems. Our minds race, our imaginations are at times like a TV screen flickering in our heads, our desires wander. To bring ourselves together it is therefore helpful to have something to focus our minds. In various methods of meditation this will vary: we have already seen the value of concentrating on scripture, on a scene in the gospels, on a mantra, on a phrase of the bible.

A very simple form of meditation, recommended by saints like Teresa of Avila, is the very slow recitation of a prayer like the *Our Father*, pondering its meaning and responding as in *lectio divina*.

In any meditation, as indeed in all prayer, there is the problem with distractions: thoughts not relevant to the meditation or prayer. The masters of the spiritual life all insist that one calmly refocuses on the topic of prayer.

These practical issues have been considered with great wisdom in the Buddhist tradition to which we now turn.

Buddhist meditation

Just as in Christianity, meditation cannot be abstracted from the coherence of Buddhist teaching and practice. One cannot here present Buddhism in all its richness.[11] Like Christianity, Buddhism too embraces a wide range of traditions in various places and in various times. Three major divisions exist: Southern (Sri Lanka and South East Asia), Eastern (China and Japan) and Northern (Tibet). Within each there are various schools and traditions. A brief outline of Buddhism, which will cover many of its forms, will allow us to see where its distinctive teaching on meditation is to be found. One might note in passing that the two classic languages of Buddhist scriptures are Pali and Sanskrit. This can lead to some confusion as people writing on the topic may transliterate from one or the other language, e.g. *nirvana* or *nibbana*.

Buddhism seeks to address the problem of universal suffering through the Four Noble Truths. First, there is the universal reality of suffering (*dukkah*) – it is not only pain and distress, but also the things that bother people, the malaise that people feel, so that life is never quite right. The second Truth is the cause of this suffering, namely desire. It can include lust for money or sensual pleasure; it is found in the gnawing dissatisfaction with what is, in craving of every kind. The Third Truth teaches that there is freedom possible where we are not dominated by greed; it is *nirvana* (*nibbana*), which is psychologically a state of great inner freedom and spontaneity, in which the mind has supreme tranquillity, purity and stability. It is the achievement of the Buddhist saints and the goal for their followers. The Fourth Noble Truth shows how this is possible, namely the Eightfold Path: right or perfect understanding, thought, action, speech, livelihood, effort, mindfulness and concentration. The first two pertain to wisdom, the next four to morality, and the final two to meditation.

Right Mindfulness and Right Concentration, the seventh and eighth items on the Eightfold Path belong to meditation. Firstly, we should seek what it means within Buddhism, and then we can examine its practice. In his well-received work on Buddhism John Snelling notes:

> Meditation is a specialized activity that helps us to fully realise the Buddha's teachings – to make them an integral part of our being rather than just a new set of ideas to be entertained theoretically in the mind. It weans

us away from our usual habit patterns, particularly our involvement with our thoughts and their emotional sub-themes. At the same time it sharpens and intensifies our powers of direct perception: it gives eyes to see into the true nature of things. The field of research is ourselves, and for this reason the laser of attention is turned and focussed inwards.

The author goes on immediately to add:

Meditation is not something to be toyed with lightly. It involves opening up the psyche and operating with it at depth. Problems, more or less difficult to handle, may arise.

He further states,

It is a misapplication of meditation to use it to obtain personal benefits – like 'mind power' or 'peak experiences.'[12]

In Buddhist mediation posture is seen as important. In Buddhism there are the postures of Yoga that promote external and internal integration.

Though in the various schools of Buddhism there is discrepancy in the use of language and terms, it can be noted that in Indian religion there is a distinction between the routes of spiritual development (*yoga*, that is 'work' or 'spiritual practice'): ritual (*karma*), devotional (*bhakti*), and meditational (*dhyana*) yoga.

There are two main schools of Buddhist meditation. One, *samatha* (tranquillity), seeks a state of calm or inner peace, brought about by overcoming disorderliness of mind or body. In this method one concentrates on a single object to the exclusion of all else. It can be one's breathing, a coloured disk or some bodily sensation. The object is ideally neutral without evoking ideas. Distraction will inevitably occur, but the meditator seeks to bring attention back to the object. Practice leads the mind to be increasingly tranquil and the ability to focus on the object of meditation for a long time without losing concentration. Some experts call this 'stabilising meditation'.

The second is *vippassana* (*vipasayana*). It is a direct experiential insight into reality, brought about by the practice of constant awareness, especially mindfulness of the four basics: body, feelings, state of mind, mental processes. There is a need to be aware of its going on inside us, an objective look which may include analysis. Thus the power of habits is lessened. It is painful to see the darker side of our nature, but that will lead to freedom. In time the meditator will come to experience three general characteristics. The first is impermanence (*anicca*): the world is in flux. The second is unsatisfactoriness, often called suffering (*dukka*), the first of the four Noble Truths. The third is insubstantiality (*anatta*): the deepest reality that is always elusive.

Though *samatha* will often be the preparation for *vippassana*, one can say that the former is more a concentration on an object with a view to simplification, whereas *vippassana* is more concerned with awareness of all of one's being as it swims before our consciousness in meditation. As it is observed, gradually the inner truth of the object and of the meditator's relation with it becomes clear. Whatever it may be, it will ultimately reflect impermanence, unsatisfactoriness and insubstantiality. These may be grasped by an insight, likened by some writers to a bolt of lightning, that momentarily illuminates all.

The aim of meditation (*dhyana yoga*) is to develop ecstasy (*samadhi*), a sort of experience of alert absorption and unification. It involves an altered or heightened state of consciousness, and has many degrees. Indian and Buddhist teachers state that exceptional states of consciousness or psychic powers are not in themselves desirable, and may hinder the traveller to *nirvana*.[13] As in Christian meditation, anything that is unusual has inherent dangers and people with such experiences have an urgent need of a wise guide.

Christian and Buddhist meditation

Since human nature is one, one will not be surprised that there are striking similarities between Christian and Buddhist meditation. Both are concerned with going beyond selfishness and failure; both have a view of suffering and the human state; both seek the good; both seek the deepest reality; both are demanding and can be life-long aims; both reject any selfish immediate pleasure and so are important in freeing people from selfishness; both offer a spiritual path which is a way of being a better person.

But there are profound differences. The syllabus expresses it adroitly: 'Buddhist meditation as an experience of emptying; Christian meditation as an experience of encounter.'[14] Even though some Christian forms of meditation use a mantra and aim at profound simplification, the ultimate aim of meditation is to make contact with God. One can say that for Catholic spirituality, unless there is a reaching for the divine, there is no prayer. The words 'reaching for' are important; very often the person praying will seem to be in dryness, darkness and finding nobody. But it is retaining the attempt to reach God that marks Christian meditation. There can be aberrations in Christian meditation when the sense of God is missing, and one is merely concentrating on breathing or on a spot, or a phrase. Christian meditation aims at surrender to God and service of others.

In recent decades the Vatican Congregation for the Doctrine of the Faith issued two warnings, available on the Vatican Internet site.[15] Both texts are concerned with ambiguities that can be present when central Christian doctrines are not explicit. In particular, the Congregation warns that prayer and meditation are ultimately a work of grace and are not merely attainable by effort. Secondly, there can be no bypassing of Jesus Christ in Christian meditation. The Christian is by baptism and conviction related to the Blessed Trinity and the whole aim of meditation is union with the God who is Three and has come to us in Jesus Christ. With these provisos the documents are open to what is good in Eastern writings.

Buddhist meditation seeks the deepest reality possible. It is *nibbana/nirvana* in all its formless beauty. The path to enlightenment is a path of denial, a refusal to rest in anything. It is ultimately a human achievement and something that the individual seeks. It is not directed towards God, as the Buddha himself (Siddharta Gautama) was rather silent, if not agnostic about a Supreme Being. There is an important social dimension in Buddhism: if one truly seeks enlightenment through following the way of the Buddha, one will be a good citizen and a source of good and compassion for all others. The practice of meditation is, however, quite individualistic. A Zen master explains meditation:

> Truth is perfect and complete in itself... Truth is not far away; it is ever present. It is not something to be attained since not one of your steps leads away from it. Do not listen to the ideas of others, but learn to listen to the voice within yourself. Your body and mind will become clear and you will realize the unity of all things. The slightest movement of your dualistic thoughts will prevent you entering the palace of meditation and wisdom... When you have thrown off your idea as to mind and body, the original truth will fully appear. Zen is simply the expression of truth; therefore longing and striving are not the true attitudes of Zen. To actualise the blessedness of meditation you should practice with pure

intention and firm determination... Do not dwell in thoughts of good and bad. Just relax and forget that you are meditating. Do not desire realisation since that thought will keep you confused... Many thoughts will crowd into your mind, ignore them, letting them go. If they persist be aware of them with the awareness, which does not think. In other words think non-thinking... In your meditation you yourself are the mirror reflecting the solution of your problems. The human mind has absolute freedom within its own nature. You can attain your freedom intuitively. Do not work for freedom, rather allow the practice itself to be liberation.[16]

The most profound difference between Buddhist and Christian meditation is, then, that the former seeks emptiness and the latter encounter with God. Buddhist meditation is a work of stern discipline, a human achievement; Christian meditation is ultimately possible only through grace.

A word about Transcendental Meditation

Transcendental Meditation (TM) is an adaptation of Hindu practices, which have traditionally been used as a way of reaching a state of oneness with the Absolute. In 1957 the Maharishi Mahesh Yogi, a Hindu monk, began to teach TM in a systematic way in the USA. It is a method for achieving deep relaxation. At the beginning it was very controversial as people were not sure about whether it was religious or not. Its founder claimed that it was not religious, but people have pointed to its roots in Hindi spirituality and the use of a mantra of uncertain meaning. Monetary payment is demanded for more advanced instruction. Scientific studies, sometimes sponsored by the TM organisation itself, claim that there are beneficial physical and psychological effects. TM is not meditation in the Christian sense. Even more perhaps than Buddhist meditation, the aim is completely centred on the well-being of the participant.

Notes

1.   *Chambers English Dictionary* (1901).

2.   *Spiritual Exercises* n. 46.

3.   Ibid., n. 54.

4.   Ibid., nn.110-117

5.   J. Main, *Word into Silence*, (London: Darton, Longman and Todd, 1980) often reprinted as in the combined volume of three of his books: *The Inner Christ, Word into Silence, The Moment of Christ, The Present Christ*, (London: Darton, Longman and Todd, 1994).

6.   See T. Keating, *Open Mind, Open Heart: the Contemplative Dimension of the Gospel* (New York: Amity House, 1986); this is reprinted along with two other books in a single volume, *Foundations for Centering Prayer and the Christian Contemplative Life– Open Mind, Open Heart – Invitation to Love – The Mystery of Christ* (New York/London: Continuum, 2002).

7.   Art., 'Centering Prayer', in *A New Dictionary of Catholic Spirituality*, ed. M. Downey, (Collegeville: Liturgical Press, 1993), pp. 138-139.

8.   B. Pennington, *Centred Living: The Way of Centering Prayer*, (Garden City NY: Doubleday, 1986/ Missouri: Liguori Press, 1999).

9.   *'Centering Prayer'*, p. 139.

10. E. Smith and J. Chalmers, *A Deeper Love: An Introduction to Centering Prayer* (London: Burns Oates, 1999).

11. For outline see P. Barnes, *World Religions. Into the Classroom* (Dublin: Veritas, 2003), pp. 140-161.

12. John Snelling, *The Buddhist Handbook: SA Complete Guide to Buddhist Teaching and Practice* (London: Century Hutchinson, 1987), p. 61.

13. Snelling, *Buddhist Handbook*, p. 66.

14. Syllabus, G. 'Worship, Prayer and Ritual' 3.1.

15. Congregation for the Doctrine of the Faith, Letter on Certain Aspects of Christian Meditation' (15 October 1989) and 'Notification concerning the Writings of Father Anthony de Mello, SJ' (24 June 1998).

16. 'Practice of Meditation' by Zen Master Dagon in J. Kornfield, and G. Fronsdal, eds. *Teachings of the Buddha* (Boston/London: Shambhala, revised and expanded 1996) pp. 150-151.

Select Bibliography

M. de Verteuil, *Let All the Peoples Praise Him: Lectio Divina and the Psalms* (Dublin: Columba, 2000).

J. Groden and C. O'Donnell, *With the Word of God: Lectio Divina. A Guide for Prayer in School, Home and Parish* (Great Wakering: McCrimmons, 2003).

C. Hayden, *Praying the Scriptures: A Practical Guide to Lectio Divina* (London: St Pauls, 2001).

E. O'Gorman and C. Kelly, *The Art of Stillness: Meditation and Relaxation in the Christian Life* (Dublin: Veritas, 1997).

E. Smith and J. Chalmers, *A Deeper Love: An Introduction to Centering Prayer* (London: Burns Oates, 1999).

On Buddhism

B.K. Hawkins, *Buddhism*. Religions of the World (London: Routledge, 1999).

J. Kornfield, and G. Fronsdal, eds. *Teachings of the Buddha* (Boston/London: Shambhala, revised and expanded 1996).

N. Smart, *The World's Religions* (Cambridge: University Press, 2nd ed. 1998).

J. Snelling, *The Buddhist Handbook: A Complete Guide to Buddhist Teaching and Practice* (London: Century Hutchinson, 1987).

9

The Contemplative Traditions

Like so many of the words we have encountered in this section of the syllabus, 'contemplation' and 'contemplative' have many possible meanings that are not easy to fix. The dictionary gives us a range of senses: to consider, to meditate, to consider attentively, and to intend. When we speak about contemplative prayer, we are indicating that it is less active than discursive or active meditation; we may also be thinking of a prayer that is very deeply graced.

There are two ways of serving God: the active life, and the contemplative life. These cannot be exclusive. The story of Martha and Mary is traditionally used to illustrate the two ways:

> Now as they went on their way, [Jesus] entered a certain village, where a woman named Martha welcomed him into her home. She had a sister named Mary, who sat at the Lord's feet and listened to what he was saying. But Martha was distracted by her many tasks; so she came to him and asked, 'Lord, do you not care that my sister has left me to do all the work by myself? Tell her then to help me.' But the Lord answered her, 'Martha, Martha, you are worried and distracted by many things; there is need of only one thing. Mary has chosen the better part, which will not be taken away from her.' (Luke 10:38-42)

Many people will have much sympathy for Martha who took the initiative of welcoming Jesus (because she was the elder?). But she is rebuked for her anxiety, and Mary is praised for her resting with Jesus and her attention to his words. Though Mary is praised for having chosen 'the better part', Martha's work is important too. Without work there would be no meal. Traditionally this text is used to support the idea that, while both active and contemplative dimensions are important, there is some priority for the contemplative. Prayer and activity are both essential for our facility and social life. Each must have a place in every person's life.

Monastic and eremitical life

From early times we find evidence of people withdrawing from society in order to commit themselves more fully to God (the Essenes in Judaism from *c.* Second century BCE to second century CE) or to seek spiritual enlightenment (the disciples of the Buddha, *c.* 500 BCE). About the end of the third century hermits began to be found in deserted places in Egypt and the Arabian Peninsula. Anthony (*c.* 250-365) became an inspirational figure when monks gathered around him for guidance. He is known as 'the father of monasticism.' In time other monastic leaders would write rules for monks beginning with Pacomius (*c.* 290-364) in the East and St Benedict (*c.* 480-547) in Europe. In these years we see a shift from eremitical living to coenobitic, that is, community living, under a superior called an Abbot (from *abba* father). Later female communities developed with an abbess. In these early forms of consecrated life there was great emphasis on prayer, on solitude, on penance and on manual work (often agriculture, basket, mat or rope-making). Here we find the main emphasis on the Mary dimension of life, but Martha who worked and was occupied is also an example.

In these communities there was great importance given to spiritual direction: they realised that one can easily be led astray, even in a desert. A protection against self-deception and diabolical illusion was to find a wise person who would help them to discern God's will. In the beginning the monasteries were very austere (as they would later be in Ireland). But in time there was a growing conviction that penance can be strict, but moderation is a key virtue. The wise monk should not err by either laxity or excessive austerity. As we might say today, the spiritual life has the demanding character of a marathon rather than the sharp exertion of a sprint.

Irish monasticism

The great monastic settlements in Ireland were very influenced by eastern models, though they also learned from western leaders like John Cassian (c. 360-after 430). There were huge communities in such places as Armagh, Kildare, Glendalough, and Clonmacnoise. They sometimes became towns with an ecclesiastical head. The Irish monasteries were centres of scholarship: Latin learning was cultivated. Scholars came from abroad to Ireland, which became known as 'the island of saints and scholars'. The work of the monasteries was varied: agriculture; the copying of and illustration of manuscripts; art in stone and metal. Later Irish monks went as pilgrim missionaries throughout Western Europe in places like Bobbio, which had an abbey founded by St Columbanus (d. 615) and Wurzburg converted by St Kilian (d. 689). From his *Confessions* we know that St Patrick had established nuns who lived in consecrated celibacy. St Brigid is, of course, the best known of the Irish nuns; she was abbess in Kildare (d. c. 525).

The local tourist office will usually be a good information resource about local monasteries and can often guide people to sites and to guides or local historians who can give authoritative information.

Two contemplative traditions

We take one male and one female contemplative tradition.

Benedictine

There is little known about the early life of St Benedict. He was born at Nursia about 480. Educated at Rome, the licentiousness of life there prompted him to withdraw from the world and he went to live as a hermit in a cave at Subiaco. About 529 he left there for Monte Cassino with a few monks. He remained there until his death about 550.

Whilst at Monte Cassino he planned a reform of monasticism and wrote a celebrated *Rule*. This was a practical plan for living that has spiritual elements as well as legislation, administrative structures and advice. The *Rule* of Benedict is characterised by wisdom and moderation. The monastery is ruled by an abbot chosen by the monks. He has full authority to govern the monastery and responsibility for the physical and spiritual well being of all the monks.

The chief task of a Benedictine monastery is the Divine Office (the *opus Dei* – work of God – now called the Liturgy of the Hours). Private prayer, study and work make up the rest of the day. Benedictines have made great contributions to liturgical scholarship, especially since the mid-nineteenth century; their work made possible many of the liturgical reform which took place after Vatican II (1962-1965). They are also involved in education at many of their monasteries. We cannot be sure if St Benedict himself ever was ordained a priest. His order includes priests and brothers; there is a separate branch for women.

Carmelite contemplatives

The Carmelite Order takes it origin from Mount Carmel, a peninsula overlooking the sea near Haifa in the Holy Land. The prophet Elijah famously overcame the followers of Baal on Mount Carmel (see 1 Kgs 18:17-46). Hermits were found near the Fountain of Elijah on Mount Carmel at various times; there was a well-established group around 1180. They sought to have a *Rule* from the local bishop, St Albert of Jerusalem, some time about 1210. These hermits were contemplatives, marked by silence, prayer, and penance. From about 1230 the Saracens made it impossible to live on Mount Carmel and the hermit brothers came to Europe; soon with the Franciscans, Dominicans and Augustinians became friars (from *frater*, a brother). The friars sought to keep a contemplative spirit along with active ministry. By the middle of the fifteenth century there were women Carmelites, who were more contemplative than the friars, being enclosed and not having any major pastoral activity.

The sixteenth century saw the Carmelite Order, along with many others, in need of reform. St Teresa of Avila reformed a branch of the Carmelite Order in Spain, which became the ODC (Order of Discalced Carmelites – discalced meaning without shoes). The Carmelite nuns in these islands all stem from the Teresian reform. Teresa stressed poverty, that is, great simplicity of lifestyle and lengthy times for private prayer – two hours per day in addition to Mass and the Liturgy of the Hours, which she insisted was to be recited in a simpler way to make time for contemplative prayer. Apart from the example and teaching of St Teresa, Carmelites find two figures as central to their spirituality: the prophet Elijah who sought and served God, and Mary who is at the heart of the Carmelite vocation.

Contemplatives today
In Ireland today there are a number of religious congregations that continue contemplative life. Since it might be possible to organise a visit to their foundations in Ireland, a list may be helpful.

Male contemplatives
The main contemplative orders of men in Ireland are of Benedictine origin. There are Benedictines, OSB, in Glenstal (Murroe). Also taking inspiration from Benedict is the Cistercian Order, OCSO, which arose from a reform in the late eleventh century at Citeaux in France. The Cistercian life is

marked by an emphasis on liturgical prayer, on manual work and on silence. Cistercian monasteries are marked by great simplicity. Houses in Ireland are found in Mount Melleray, Roscrea, Mellifont (Collon), Bolton Abbey (Moone), and Portglenone (Ballymena).

Female contemplatives

There are three main traditions of contemplative nuns. There is a Cistercian Abbey in Glencairn (Co. Waterford) and a Benedictine monastery at Kylemore (Co. Mayo). Secondly, there is a Franciscan Contemplative Order called the Poor Clares (not to be confused with the Sisters of St Clare, who are an active congregation). The Poor Clares who live by a Franciscan simplicity are found in Belfast, Galway City, Carlow, Cork, Ennis, Drumshambo and Ballsbridge in Dublin. Thirdly, there are Carmelite nuns following the Carmelite Rule as adopted by St Teresa of Avila (d. 1582). Houses in Ireland are in Delgany (Co. Wicklow), Knock, Loughrea, New Ross, Newry and Tallow; as well as Dublin – Firhouse, Hampton (Drumcondra), Kilmacud (Stillorgan), Malahide, and Roebuck (Clonskeagh). In addition there are Dominican contemplatives in Drogheda, Visitandines (Stamullan, Co. Meath) and Perpetual Adoration Sisters (Wexford Town).

Many contemplative women live in enclosure: the convent has private areas which outsiders are not allowed to visit. It is neither to keep the sisters in, nor to keep the world out. It provides rather a space and a freedom, the silence and peace that the contemplative life needs. It cuts out the noise and bustle of the world, but at the same time allows the nuns to become involved with the world and its pain at a very deep level, Members do not ordinarily change from one monastery to another. They have strict vows and are called 'nuns'. All other women religious are more properly called 'sisters'. The Family of Adoration Sisters at Ferns are a contemplative congregation, but are not enclosed. Finally, one should note the Carmelite hermits of men and women at the Holy Hill Hermitage, Skreen, Co. Sligo.

The meaning of contemplative life

Religious vocation is a call to follow Christ. Many congregations reflect Christ's care for the poor, for those in physical or psychological need, for those who are in some sense ill. Others answer his call to go to preach to all nations (Matt 28:18-20). In their retirement and prayer, contemplative religious follow Christ who spent time alone in worship of his Father. Contemplatives speak of their vocation as somehow a totality of giving; they speak of the simplicity of their lives and offering; above all they speak of responding to God's love. These ideas are not peculiar to contemplatives; people in the world and family life may share them. But in the case of contemplatives, there is intensity in their desires, a single-mindedness that is very difficult to have in the wider society. Contemplative life is simple; it is far from easy. Only a profound love for God and for the world makes sense of this life. They are a reminder of the primacy of God and for the need to find in God the meaning of all our lives. Contemplatives are a powerful reminder to the rest of the Church that happiness does not ultimately lie in things or in achievements but in loving and being loved. Contemplatives spend a lot of time in prayer, but they also work. They want to give themselves totally to God in a way that will serve the Church. Simple people grasp this, and constantly go to contemplative monasteries seeking prayer or guidance in their lives.

Highly successful and gifted people go aside to find God and to serve the world in another way. The Jewish philosopher Edith Stein (1891-1942) first became a Catholic and then gave up an enormously important lecturing career in Nazi Germany to join the Carmelite Order in 1934. In doing so she was convinced that she was serving God, serving society and assisting her own beloved Jewish people. She went to the gas chambers of Auschwitz still holding this conviction. She was canonised as a martyr in 1998.

Retreat

In the contemplative traditions that we have examined, we see values that are important for any reflective Christian life. Only very few people have a calling to spend their whole lives as contemplatives. In chapter four we have already looked at the need for reflection in a healthy mature life. In our search for God we also need space for reflection. This setting time aside, often in a special place, is traditionally called a 'retreat' (from Latin 'withdraw' or 'draw back'). Christians often look at the example of Jesus who went to the desert to reflect after he was anointed as suffering Messiah at his Baptism in the Jordan. He spent forty days (Hebrew expression for a long time) in the desert where he engaged in spiritual battle against the Tempter (see Matt 3; Luke 3; Mark 1). He came out of the desert experience 'in the power of the Spirit' and began his public ministry (Luke 4:14-21).

This practice of going apart has a long history in Christian tradition. Many people take a few days, a weekend, or a day or two to reflect. Any sensible travellers on an important journey will pause occasionally, rest and reflect on how they are going – looking back over their journey, examining their present position and looking to the future. A retreat, even if short, can be a contemplative experience. A retreat is a time for prayer, perhaps for considering one's relationship with God, for repentance, for good resolutions, for thanksgiving. All this takes place in a quiet atmosphere; without some quiet a retreat cannot succeed. But there can also be dialogue and sharing with others, common prayer and reflection. But what is essential is that people look at their lives and desires, bringing them before God's mercy and his power. A retreat is thus a time to consider again the gifts of Confirmation and the need that people have for the Holy Spirit in their lives.

Retreats are of many kinds. It is good to experience several kinds; indeed one that a person may not have liked at first can do them more good than a more attractive period. Some retreats emphasise good input, which can guide one's lives. Others can be quieter in which there is more time alone. There are many activities that can help us to slow down, to relax, to reflect, such as quiet non-demanding work, art-work that has a sacred or personal focus; walking, sitting, enjoying nature, visiting a Church or sacred place. Any of these can help people to move easily into a more contemplative mould.

School retreats are an area perhaps needing some careful reflection at this time. One problem is that they can be seen, especially by teenagers, as imposed on them. Another difficulty is the level of expectation from the pupils and from the teachers. Some retreats may only enhance adolescent self-absorption. They may be superficial with excessive emphasis on music, role-play and what young people like. Retreats cannot be just at an emotional level; there is an intellectual content to the Christian faith. One must of course meet people where they are. It would seem, however, that for a Christian school retreat to be meaningful, it needs to challenge young people with three questions for reflection: who are you? Who is Christ? How are the two related? These questions in the Catholic context should flow naturally into an experience of reconciliation and of Eucharistic celebration. A retreat time is one for making life choices and for evaluating the choices that people have made in the recent or not so recent past

Hermitage

We have seen that the first indications of religious life in the third century were hermits who went to deserted places in the desert. The word 'hermit' ultimately comes from the Greek word for desert, *erêmia*. There have always been people who go off to live alone for longer or shorter periods. There were many hermits in early Irish Christianity. Inevitably people came to seek their wisdom and the hermit was no longer alone, but in charge of a monastery that grew up around him, even on a place as inhospitable as Skellig Rock off the Iveragh peninsula Co. Kerry. St Francis found medieval Assisi at times to be too frenetic and he used to go up the mountain to a retreat cell called the *Carcere*. In Ireland today and in Europe generally one encounters the occasional hermit living in a city or in a rural area. These are people who are seeking God in solitude; if their calling is authentic they will also be deeply committed to praying for the Church and the deep needs of the world. Hermits generally have no uniform rule of life, but they may choose a spiritual tradition, such as the Benedictine or Carmelite one to guide and mould their lives.

In the past few decades we have seen the emergence of hermitages where people can go for a time of reflection. These are often simple, self-contained units where people can have quiet in a religious atmosphere. There are hermitages in Ferns, Co Wexford, at Laragh near Glendalough and others attached to various religious communities and retreat houses.

In the 1970s a Russian emigrée, Catherine de Hueck Doherty, opened a *poustinia* in the archdiocese of Toronto[1]. She married Baron de Hueck about 1917. After the October revolution of 1917 they fled and arrived penniless in Canada. Her husband died rather soon thereafter. Her fortunes picked up and she became quite wealthy. She felt a call to renounce her riches and went to live in the slums of Toronto establishing a Friendship House where poor people could meet and find shelter. She later remarried to Eddie Doherty, a well-known journalist. Eventually the vision of the Friendship House became that of Madonna Houses that were loosely structured but highly committed lay communities. She saw herself as living the simplicity of Nazareth. Catherine remained deeply influenced by the spirituality of the Russian Church. It had a tradition for hermits (*poustinik*, pl. *poustinikki*) to go away 'to pray to God for their sins and the sins of the world, to atone, to fast, to live in poverty, and to enter the great silence of God.'[2] She chose the word *poustinia*, meaning 'desert' to describe the simple hut in which people went aside for prayer, fasting and reflection. It was to contain some bedding, a table, chair and bible, some paper and a pencil. Facilities were the simplest. There was a simple cross without a figure so that people could envisage themselves on it. The hut finally had an icon of Our Lady and a lamp. The *poustinia*, she used to say, was a place for resting in the Lord. She insisted more and more that the true *poustinia* does not depend on being in a remote area. The true *poustinia* is the desert of the heart. The place can be an attic, a spare room, a cupboard, a quite corner of a room; it is a place to seek God and to open one's heart to him. The vision of Catherine was eagerly taken up in the 1980s and later; the word '*poustinia*' became used for a hermitage. But such facilities may not have the original inspiration of Catherine.

Pilgrimage

Pilgrimages are journeys to holy places. The motivation can be to seek a divine favour, to do penance or in thanksgiving. The word 'pilgrim' comes from a Latin word *peregrinus,* which means a stranger, or perhaps a resident alien. The idea is that of Christians being 'strangers and pilgrims' on earth (see Heb 11:13), with their true citizenship being in heaven (see Ph 3:20; Eph 2:19). Pilgrimages can be a visit to a holy place; there has also been a tradition in the Irish Church of life pilgrimage for the love of God, in which people set out like Abraham (see Gen 12:1) without clear destination but trusting in God. For some young people voluntary work overseas can have this meaning.

The idea of holy places and of pilgrimage is found in many religions. Some places associated with great religious figures are felt to be especially sacred, so that visiting them can in some sense put one in touch with holy persons. Thus we have Hindu and Buddhist holy places; for Islam there is the *hajj* pilgrimage to Mecca. In the early Church people set out to visit the places where the Lord and his disciples walked. A devout woman from

Spain or possibly Gaul set out on pilgrimage to the Holy Land and monastic sites in Egypt and the Arabian desert about 381-384. Her travelogue, *Egeria's Pilgrimage*, recounts what she witnessed in monastic life and in liturgy; it is an invaluable historical record. She was just one of thousands, but fortunately she wrote up her experiences, perhaps for the nuns in her monastery back home.

By the Middle Ages there were three great pilgrimage centres: the Holy Land, the tombs of Sts Peter and Paul at Rome and Santiago de Compostela, the reputed burial place of the apostle James. People also came to Canterbury from all around Europe to pray at the tomb of St Thomas Becket, martyred in 1170 on the orders of Henry II. The pilgrim way from London or Winchester to Canterbury can still be traced; it has been immortalised in Chaucer's *Canterbury Tales*. In the Middle Ages making a pilgrimage might be imposed as a penance for very grave sins.

In addition to travel to foreign shrines the spiritual life has often been compared to a pilgrimage. In English there is *The Pilgrim's Progress* by John Bunyan (1622-88), an allegory of the journey to God of a man called Christian, his wife and children. Many spiritual writers like St Teresa of Avila and John of the Cross speak of the inner journey in which a person seeks God as a pilgrimage. Vatican II refers to 'the pilgrimage of faith' of the Blessed Virgin that began at the Annunciation and ended at the holy place of Calvary, where she stood beneath the Cross.[3]

In Ireland there are many pilgrimages. There are always holy places nearby, often a well that people may visit on the feast of the saint, like the well of St Declan in Ardmore (Co. Waterford), where people gather for the 24 July. In these sites there is often what is called a 'station', namely a set of prayers and exercises performed at the holy place; one frequently encounters some ascetical element like going barefoot. Well-known places of pilgrimage all year round are Our Lady's Island (Co. Wexford), and Knock (Co. Mayo). There are three major pilgrimage places associated with our National Apostle: Croagh Patrick, or the

Reek (Co. Mayo), his grave at Downpatrick (Co. Down), and the penitential pilgrimage island of Lough Derg (Co. Donegal). There are also many places associated with his memory, such as wells, places where he preached, baptised and rested. Local historians, or perhaps tourist information offices, will be able to indicate holy places and pilgrimage sites relatively near any school in Ireland.

Pilgrimages still draw people

At the beginning of this section we have indicated some of the reasons why people might undertake a pilgrimage, such as thanksgiving, intercession or penance. But there are many other motives. People like to travel. Whereas pilgrimage was in earlier times a lengthy and difficult journey, now one can drive to any Irish pilgrimage site in a few hours, or fly to Lourdes in two hours. The strain is certainly removed. It is thus harder to get into a pilgrimage mood and to think about where we are going, as we arrive soon after we set out. The physical difficulty of climbing Croagh Patrick and the asceticism associated with Lough Derg still allow for a pilgrim spirit.

In its *Directory on Popular Piety,* The Vatican Congregation for Divine Worship (2001) indicates some key ideas still applicable to contemporary pilgrimages. It states that 'Despite change, pilgrimage has maintained the essential traits of its spirituality throughout the ages, down to our own time.' It then notes five dimensions of pilgrimage:

> *Eschatological Dimension.* The original and essential quality of pilgrimage: a pilgrimage, or 'journey to a shrine', is both a moment in and parable of, our journey towards the Kingdom; it affords an opportunity for the Christian to take greater stock of one's eschatological destiny... journeying between the obscurity of the faith... and the desire for everlasting life... between frenetic activity and contemplation.

Penitential dimension. Pilgrimage is also a journey of conversion: in journeying towards a shrine pilgrims move from a realisation of their own sinfulness and of their attachment to ephemeral and unnecessary things to interior freedom and an understanding of the deeper meaning of life.

Festive dimension. The penitential aspect of pilgrimage is complemented by a festive aspect: the festive dimension also lies at the heart of pilgrimage, and arises from many anthropological reasons.... A pilgrimage can be a break from the monotony of daily routine; it can be an alleviation of the burdens of everyday life, especially for the poor whose lot is heavy; it is an occasion to give expression to Christian fraternity, in moments of friendship meeting each other, and spontaneity which can sometimes be repressed.

Worship dimension. Pilgrimage is essentially an act of worship: a pilgrim goes to a shrine to encounter God, to be in his presence, and to offer him adoration in worship, and to open his heart to him. During his visit to the shrine, the pilgrim completes many acts of worship that are properly liturgical or drawn from popular piety. Frequently, the pilgrim's prayers are directed to Our Lady, or to the Angels and Saints who are regarded as powerful intercessors with God. The icons venerated at pilgrim shrines are signs of the presence of the Mother of God and the Saints who surround the Lord in his glory, 'living for ever to intercede for us' (Hb 7, 25), and always present in the community gathered in his name (see Mt 18: 20; 28: 20). Sacred images, whether of Christ, his Mother, the Angels and Saints, are signs of the divine presence and of God's provident love; they bear witness to the prayers of generations raised up to God in supplication, to the sighs of the afflicted, and to the thankful joy of those who have received grace and mercy.

Apostolic dimension. The pilgrim's journey, in a certain sense, recalls the journey of Christ and his disciples as they travelled throughout Palestine to announce the Gospel of salvation. In this perspective, pilgrimage is a proclamation of faith in which pilgrims become 'errant heralds of Christ' (414).

Dimension of communion. The pilgrims who journey to a shrine are in a communion of faith and charity not only with those who accompany them on the 'sacred journey' (see Luke 24: 13-35) but also with the Church in heaven and on earth. They travel with all of the faithful who have prayed at that shrine down through the centuries. They appreciate the natural beauty that surrounds the shrine.[4]

Conclusion

We began with the story of Martha and Mary. The contemplative dimension is in some ways more important. It is from sitting at the feet of Jesus that people learn how to order their lives, and to be active in an effective and focused way. God is served by both contemplative and active life. The contemplative dimension of life, however, does not just happen. It is necessary to make provision by allowing time, space, environment and circumstances for the contemplative dimension of life. Cardinal Hume once wrote that with a candle and an icon he could make children contemplative. The candle provides the sacred time and space; the icon represents a divine truth, the focus for a contemplative vision. With so many people convinced of the need for reflection in contemporary society, the great religions have a wisdom about it that can well serve society and help to redeem it from greed, hyperactivity, superficial goals and material success.

Notes

1. C. de Hueck Doherty, *Poustinia: Christian Spiritualit of the East for Western Man* (London: Collins Books, 1975) p. 33.
2. Ibid., p. 1-7
3. See Vatican II, *Constitution on the Church*, LG 58.
4. *Directory* n. 286 [some sentences have been changed to plural to maintain inclusive language.]

Select Bibliography

And Speak to Her Heart: The Vocation of Contemplative Nuns (Dublin: Conference of Major Religious Superiors, 1983).

David Alton, *Pilgrim Ways* (London: St Paul, 2001). Pilgrim sites in United Kingdom and Ireland.

Congregation for Divine Worship, *Directory on Popular Piety and the Liturgy: Principles and Guidelines* (Libreria Editrice Vatican, 2002). Available on Vatican website.

J. Duffy, *Patrick in His Own Words* (Dublin: Veritas, 2000).

D. Flanagan, ed., *The Meaning of Knock* (Dublin: Columba Press, 1997). Articles on various aspects of Knock including 'The Meaning of Pilgrimage' by M. Drumm.

J. Groden, *St Patrick: Spirit and Prayer* (Great Wakering: McCrimmons, 2002. A booklet with a short account of Patrick and his prayer and illustrations of Patrician sites.

E. Healy, *In Search of Ireland's Holy Wells* (Dublin: Wolfhound, 2001). A delightful illustrated and popular account of the author's travels to many Irish wells.

T. O'Loughlin, *St Patrick: The Man and His Works* (London: SPCK/Triangle Books, 1999).

N. Pennick, *The Celtic Saints: An Illustrated and Authoritative Guide to these Extraordinary Men and Women* (New York: Sterling, 1997).

P. Sheldrake, *Living Between Worlds: Place and Journey in Celtic Spirituality* (London: Darton, Longman and Todd, 1995).

The Mystic Traditions

In modern times the word 'mysticism' can be found used in widely differing ways. Indeed, it is hard to find a territory of culture in which one will not come across the word: music, art, literature, economics, science... The meaning varies from culture to culture, sometimes with highly evocative if hazy meanings ('scholasticism of the heart, the dialect of feelings' – J.W. Goethe), at other times with descriptive definitions that are almost impossible to penetrate. In general, one can say that wherever one finds a search for the absolute or for what is ineffable, one can find the word 'mysticism': in the great world religions, in Celtic spirituality often tinged with New Age, in various forms of Wicca, in ecology, in art... But especially we find the word used about peak experiences: the late quartets of Beethoven, the poetry of William Blake, hallucinatory drugs, out of body encounters, New Age experiences, aesthetics and so forth.

A problem word

The Anglican, Dean William Ralph Inge, wrote in 1899, 'No word in our language – not even Socialism – has been employed more loosely than "mysticism"', and he listed and criticised twenty-six definitions of mysticism and mystical theology. The word is still often unclear. The American Dominican expert on spirituality,

Jordan Aumann, suggests the reason for such multiplicity: 'the data of mystical experience is vague and lacks precision because the experience is indescribable.'[1] However, there is in recent years some growth of convergence among Christian authors.[2]

The adjective 'mystical' (Greek *mystikos*) does not appear in the Scriptures. There is a closely aligned word, 'mystery' (*mystêrion*). Both are etymologically related to the verb *muô*, which has the sense of closing lips or eyes. The Greeks had mysteries, *mystika*, which were religions and cults whose initiated were known as *hoi mystai/mystikoi*. Hence, there is a foundational idea of what is secret or hidden, a meaning found also in the scriptures (e.g. Dan 2:28; Matt 13:11; I Cor 2:7; Eph 1:9' 3:9; Rom 16:25).[3]

In the patristic period beginning with Origen we find 'mystical' used of the hidden sense of scripture revealed in the coming of Christ. The term 'mystical' was used about the sacraments, especially the Eucharist. The Latin Fathers often used the word 'contemplation' where modern authors might use 'mysticism'. By the later Middle Ages there is a growing consensus that 'mystical theology' by whatever name referred to knowledge of God attained by direct, immediate and ineffable contemplation.[4] It is thus distinguished from 'natural theology', knowledge of God from creatures, often through philosophical reflection, and from 'dogmatic theology' which is knowledge of God from revelation. It is helpful to have as points of reference three definitions cited by H.D. Egan:[5]

- 'The raising of the mind to God through the desire of love' (St Bonaventure, d. 1274).
- 'The experimental knowledge of God through the embrace of unitive love' (John Gerson, d. 1429).
- 'Contemplation is the mystical theology which theologians call secret wisdom which St Thomas says is communicated and infused into the soul through love' (St John of the Cross, d. 1592).

To which we could add:

- 'Mysticism is wisdom or knowledge that is found through love; it is loving knowledge.' (William Johnston, an Irish Jesuit who has spent most of his life in Japan bringing together Christianity and Buddhism).[6]

Egan makes two important points about these classical definitions. Firstly, they indicate an experience of God that is somehow direct, immediate, intuitive and beyond the normal workings of the intellect and senses. To use the language of the fourth chapter, mysticism is a depth experience, but it is more. It is a profound religious experience in which mystics enter into self-transcendence. Mystics often unite the two words, 'love and knowledge.'

William James

With his book, *The Varieties of Religious Experience*,[7] William James was one of the first to approach mysticism as an independent phenomenon that cannot be reduced to other psychological phenomena. James is considered as the father of modern religious psychology. His book remains a classic with enormous influence on all that followed him. He was probably the first to make the distinction 'once-born'/'twice-born' religious types.

James is especially remembered for his four marks of mystical experience:

It is *ineffable* in that it must be directly experienced in order to be understood – only one who has been in love really understands a lover's experience.

It is *noetic* (intellectual from *noein* to think) conveying some state of knowledge or awareness that transcends the discursive intellect.

It is *transitory* in that the experience passes, even though a succession of experiences changes a person.

It is *passive,* not open to be striven for, in order to be acquired; it always has the notion of gift.

It is usually pointed out that these categories are too broad to specify mystical experience successfully. We can have many experiences that are ineffable; we have experiences in which we come into new awareness or knowledge; we have many transitory experiences; we feel at times that an experience just comes to us, that it is not the fruits of our efforts, unlike say seeing at last a theorem in geometry. An American pragmatist in all his writing, James' great achievement was perhaps to give the lie to the assumption of previous psychologists that mystics were deviant, odd or the victims of self-hypnosis or autosuggestion.

Evelyn Underhill

A more profound and successful attempt to come to terms with mysticism is the Anglican laywoman, Evelyn Underhill (Mrs Stuart Moore). Her study, *Mysticism: The Nature and Development of Spiritual Consciousness* (1911),[8] remains one of the classics of mystical theology, and is still valuable. Like James, she adopted a descriptive method and used texts from Christian and non-Christian tradition. The key insight of her work is the distinction between the 'mystic fact' and the 'mystic way.' Under the former she shows how mysticism relates to philosophical systems, to psychology, symbolism and magic; she also gives the characteristics of mysticism. Under the latter she considers mysticism as part of a life process and not a matter of transient experiences or occasional visions. It is rather a movement towards perfect union with the God of Love.

She noted three major symbols or cravings of the mystics: the craving that makes the mystic a wanderer, a pilgrim, who goes out in search of a lost home or better country; the craving of heart for heart, that makes the mystic a lover; the craving for inner purity and perfection that makes the mystic an ascetic and in the end, a saint.[9] She speaks of a trinity of experiences: mysticism is an act of love, which is common to many religions;

it is an act of supreme perception, the mystic sees, understands, is a visionary; it is an act of surrender to God. It is when the three are found together that we may be encountering mysticism.

Again, more clearly than James, she grasped that mysticism is not concerned primarily with peak experiences, altered states of consciousness, or even with self-actualisation. It is the living God who initiates the mystic's search. As such it is distinct from magic for 'magic wants to get, mysticism wants to give.'[10]

For Underhill there are five marks of genuine Christian mysticism, characteristics that can be found to a great extent in the mysticism of other religions too:

1. Mysticism is *practical and active*, not passive and theoretical. It is an organic life-process, which engages the whole person: 'Their [the mystics'] favourite symbols are those of action: battle, search, pilgrimage... Those who suppose mystical experience to be merely a pleasing consciousness of the Divine in the world, a sense of the 'otherness' of things, a basking in the beams of Uncreated Light are only playing with reality.'[11]

2. Mysticism is an entirely *transcendental and spiritual activity*: 'It is in no way concerned with doing, exploring, re-arranging, or improving anything in the physical universe... Though [the Mystic] does not, as his enemies declare, neglect his duty to the many, his heart is always upon the changeless One.'[12] The mystic's experience of God annihilates all desire for knowledge, happiness, virtue or occult power. On the quest the mystic may indeed seek knowledge, but ultimately the genuine mystic wants only God, and everything less is subsumed or left aside.

3. *Only love explains mysticism*; the mystic is essentially a lover. The mystic does not seek Reality as an object, but as personal and living. It is love that distinguishes the mystic from the

philosopher, the poet, the artist, and the magician. 'I saw Him
and sought Him: I had Him and wanted Him.'[13] The
fourteenth-century English mystical treatise, *The Cloud of
Unknowing*, states: 'God can certainly be loved, not thought; he
can be taken and held by love not knowing.'[44]

4. Mysticism entails a definite *psychological experience,* it results
   in a qualitatively transformed life; the encounter with
   Absolute holiness demands and brings about conversion, a
   rebuilding of the self on higher levels.

5. One can add, or see as a summary, that true mysticism *is
   never self-seeking.* The mystic lives out the Gospel saying that
   it is by losing life that we gain it.

The other major contribution of Underhill is her description of
the phases or stages of the mystical life. Basing herself on
Teresa of Avila (mainly *The Interior Castle/Mansions*) she
outlines five stages.

1. *The Awakening of the Self to the consciousness of the Divine
   Reality.* In a wide diversity of ways, sometimes through
   consolation and desolation, through joy and unrest, or
   perhaps without any crisis at all, the person's centre of
   gravity is displaced and a process of conversion begins.

2. Then follows *the purification of the self.* There is a painful
   awareness of the contrast between God's holiness, beauty
   and being, and the sinfulness of the creature.

3. The third stage that follows purification is *the illumination of
   the self.*[15] This stage, which many never pass beyond, has
   many dimensions. Some would regard this stage as the first
   truly mystic stage. It is marked by various experiences, such
   as: a deep sense of the divine presence; a sense of union

with God, but which is not yet complete; an intuition of God's plans for the world; the world is seen from God's point of view; a manifold gifting of various mystical gifts all of which are in some sense a self-revelation of God.

4. Between the illuminative way that she calls 'the first mystic life' and the unitive or 'the second mystic life', Underhill deals with *the dark night of the soul*. We need to be careful to allow that God may work his grace-filled purification using also the psychological state of the person. The aim of this state of purification is the total transformation of the person, the elimination of all that is of sin and selfishness and the establishment of utter purity of mind and heart. This stage of the Dark Night of the Soul is a final purification of self-love and prepares for the final stage of the mystic life.

5. The last stage is called by Underhill the 'Unitive Life'.[16] There is a variety of symbolic language for this state: deification, transformation into God by participation, full divine union. This is the highest of the mystic states. Underhill is critical of Eastern mystics who seek a higher stage still of self-loss or annihilation, but she may not have fully grasped their symbolism and may have failed to see the Spirit truly at work in mystics of non-Christian traditions.

From Underhill we see something of the complexity of the mystic search. It is ultimately not the mystic's search for God, but God's search for the mystic, who then surrenders to divine love. But there is a problem in the fact that deep levels of selfishness and inauthenticity lie in us all. This must be healed, purified, restored. We need, as noted above, a decentring: from looking at ourselves and our desires, we have to look much more towards God and the needs of others. In this we will ultimately find our joy and happiness.

How do we consider people like Simone Weil and Dag Hammarskjöld, whose unusual and attractive spirituality seems to lack the transformation and purification found in mainstream mystics? Harvey D. Egan notes, 'The interpretation of their own loneliness and experience of God may be an attractive form of contemporary spirituality, but it is not Christian mysticism.'[17]

Karl Rahner

One of the most important Catholic theologians of the twentieth century was Karl Rahner. He sought to begin theology from experience, to invite people to see in their experience a calling to something higher, of a desire for what will ultimately satisfy. His student and contemporary authority on mysticism, Harvey D. Egan wrote:

> Central to his thinking is the view that at the core of every person's deepest experience, what haunts every human heart, is a God whose mystery, light and love have embraced the total person. God works in every person's life as the One to whom everybody must freely say his or her yes or no. We may deny this, ignore it, repress it, but deep down we know that God is in love with us and that we are all, at least secretly, in love with each other.[18]

He is particularly famous for his saying, 'The Christian of the future will be a mystic or will not exist at all.'[19] He points to life experiences, what we have been calling religious depth experiences, in which a person deeply conscious of his or her weakness makes an act of commitment to love, to obey, to forgive, to hold on in dark faith, to surrender to God's way. Here there is true mysticism, a search and a reaching towards God, with new perspectives and love.

The mystic's experience

A constant theme in almost every chapter has been the problem of language, its inadequacy to communicate experience. In the case of the mystics, it is immeasurably compounded. Very often the mystic will use paradox, poetry, even apparently contradictory language. The Spanish mystic, St John of the Cross (d. 1591), attempts to describe initial union with God:

> My Beloved the mountains,
> And lonely wooded valleys,
> Strange islands,
> And resounding rivers,
> The whistling of love-stirring breezes.
>
> The tranquil night
> At the time of the rising dawn,
> Silent music,
> Sounding solitude,
> The supper that refreshes,
> and deepens love.[20]

In the writings of the mystics we find a continual theme: the mystic has a profound sense of knowledge and love, something that is pure gift and total joy. But with this very experience there is also a still greater sense of God or the Absolute being totally Other and beyond all knowing. The key mystic experience can thus be characterised by seeking, some reaching which leads into ever-deeper even painful longing.

In the mystics we find two different ways of knowing God. Some are aware of great light from God, profound insights and knowledge. Such knowledge is called *kataphatic* (positive). There is also knowledge of God that is dark and obscure; the person is so overwhelmed by God's Being that they are blinded. In Tom Kilroy's play, *Talbot's Box*, the central character, Matt Talbot, a reformed alcoholic and mystic, is asked by Church authorities what he sees in his long hours praying in Church. He replies, 'I see nothing, but God does be in the nothing.' This way of knowing God is called *apophatic* (negative). Similarly, in a Raidió Éireann short story by Aidan Matthew, *The Figure on the Cross,* the young boy Freddy was asked by the more sympathetic of two priests, what was going on between him and a life-sized crucifix. He replied, 'If you don't know, I can't tell you.'

We can find examples of this double kind of knowing and of the mystic's search in all the mystical traditions. The difficulty of explaining the experience of the mystics can be illustrated in a secular context. When Mike Barry from Co. Kerry walked to the South Pole in January 2004, he was asked on the radio, 'Why did you do it?' He replied, 'If you have to ask the question, you won't understand the answer.'

There is a lot of contemporary psychological study of the mystics' experience. We can identify the mental processes, and see what part of the brain is operating. We can see that some of their experiences are to be found from various causes. But what is beyond psychology is the mystics' union and love of God. We may speak of the effects of mysticism on the psyche of the person; psychology will not tell us whether or not they are in loving knowledge with the Absolute Holy One. The ultimate test for the genuineness of mystical experience is the Gospel one: 'You will know them by their fruits' (Matt 7:16). Genuine mysticism shows itself in works of love, and in virtuous living.

Christian mystics

In the Christian mystical tradition, especially among Roman Catholics, mysticism is never divorced from the life of the Church. Mystics rejoice in the sacraments, especially Reconciliation and Eucharist; they treasure God's word in the bible; they are fully integrated with the cares and joys of the Christian community.

We have noted that the word mysticism does not occur in the scriptures. Yet there is much mystical writing in the Old and the New Testament. We find something of the mystic's search in many of the Psalms, e.g. Psalm 84 that expresses the Israelite's desire to be in the temple of the Lord:

> How lovely is your dwelling place,
> Lord God of hosts.
> My soul is longing and yearning,
> Is yearning for the courts of the Lord.
> My heart and my soul ring out their joy
> To God, the living God.
> The sparrow herself finds a home
> And the swallow a nest for her brood;
> She lays her young by your altars,
> Lord of hosts, my king and my God.

Paul, speaking of the transformation of his life, is quite characteristic of the Christian mystics:

> For through the law I died to the law, so that I might live to God. I have been crucified with Christ; and it is no longer I who live, but it is Christ who lives in me. And the life I now live in the flesh I live by faith in the Son of God who loved me and gave himself for me (Gal 2:19-20).

St Augustine (d. 430) recounts his conversion and spiritual journey in a passage that finds parallels in many mystical traditions:

> Late have I loved you, Beauty so old and so new: late have I loved you. And see, you were within and I was in the external world and sought you there, and in my unlovely state I plunged into those lovely created things which you made. You were with me, and I was not with you. The lovely things kept me far from you, though if they did not have their existence in you, they would have no

existence at all. You called and cried out aloud and shattered my darkness. You were radiant and resplendent, you put to flight my blindness. You were fragrant, and I drew in my breath and now pant after you. I tasted you, and I feel hunger and thirst for you. You touched me, and I am set on fire to attain the peace which is yours.[21]

Here we have the great mystical theme of both God and the human engaged in a mutual search.

Some stanzas of St John of the Cross illustrate the paradoxes involved in dark knowing when he describes an ecstasy in high contemplation:

> I entered into unknowing
> And there I remained unknowing,
> Transcending all knowledge.
>
> I entered into unknowing
> Yet when I saw myself there
> Without knowing where I was
> I understood great things;
> I shall not say what I felt
> For I remained in unknowing
> Transcending all knowledge.
>
> I was so whelmed,
> So absorbed and withdrawn,
> That my senses were left
> Deprived of all their sensing,
> And my spirit was given
> An understanding while not understanding,
> Transcending all knowledge.

Here we see the poet mystic straining with language. Our attempt to grasp his thought may open us to a different type of religious experience, or to a memory of some deep experiences that we have had, which we may be comfortable to speak about, or not have adequate language to express. At other times he speaks in ecstatic language piling up images in an effort to overcome the limitations of language. The state of union with God defies description:

> 'Let us go forth to behold ourselves in your beauty.' This means: let us so act that by means of this loving activity we may attain to the vision of ourselves in your beauty in eternal life. That is: That I be so transformed in your beauty that we may be alike in beauty, and both behold ourselves in your beauty, possessing then your very beauty; this, in such a way that each looking at the other may see in the other their own beauty, since both are your beauty alone, I being absorbed in your beauty; hence I shall see you in your beauty, and you will see me in your beauty, and I shall see myself in you in your beauty, and you will see yourself in me in your beauty; that I may resemble you in your beauty, and you resemble me in your beauty, and my beauty be your beauty and your beauty my beauty; wherefore I shall be you in your beauty, and you will be me in your beauty, because your very beauty will be my beauty; and thus we shall behold each other in your beauty.[22]

If we seek to follow the text, we will see that John of the Cross is here skating on very thin ice: many mystics have gone astray by not observing the infinite distance between God and the creature. Since all is God's gift and in God, John does not overstep this vital boundary.

Jewish mysticism

Jewish religion is very much centred on God's law. Obedience to God is even greater than sacrifice:

> He has told you O mortal, what is good; and what does the Lord require of you but to do justice, and to love kindness, and to walk humbly with your God (Mic 6:8).

Jews worship the one God, creator of the world, all knowing, ever present, tempering justice and mercy.[23] Jewish religion is practical in its worship and in its commitment to *mitzvoth*, the commandments and ritual norms that direct every moment of a traditional Jew's life. But there are many mystical traditions in Judaism which show how one can attain to profound knowledge of creation and of God, the unutterable One.[24] Many Jewish mystics speak of ascent, some finding deep meanings of the chariot in Ezekiel (ch. 1). They speak about ecstatic experiences in which the mystic in some sense leaves the world but returns to it. They emphasise the need for asceticism, for purity of heart, mind and body. One of the best-known mystical schools is the *Kabbalah* (tradition), which is found in Provence and northern Spain (*c.* 1150-1300). For the German Jewish mystics of the twelfth and early thirteenth century a key search is the life of piety (*hasidut*), whence *hasid*, a pious person seeking devotion, holiness and contemplation. From this school comes the *Hymn of Glory* that is still used in Jewish worship:

> Sweet hymns and songs will I recite
> To sing to Thee by day and night
> Of Thee who art my soul's delight.
>
> How doth my soul within me yearn
> Beneath Thy shadow to return,
> The Secret mysteries to learn.

They glory will my discourse be,
In images I picture thee,
Although myself I cannot see.

In mystic utterances alone,
By prophet and by seer made known,
Hast Thou Thy radiant glory shone.

My meditation day and night,
May it be pleasant in Thy sight,
For Thou art my soul's delight.[25]

It is particularly through its many mystics that we can glimpse at the extraordinary tenacity of Judaism and its survival even despite centuries of persecution: God constantly draws and enlightens one who seeks him above all else. Later some Kabbalistic writings would become very obscure, and in some cases deviant, wandering into the occult.

Islamic mysticism

Islam almost from the beginning has had very important mystical traditions. This ought not to surprise us, if we recall the five pillars of Islam: God is One and his prophet is Muhammad; ritual prayer, social taxation, the Ramadan fast and the Hajj pilgrimage to Mecca. Islam has a deep sense of the sacred; the Qur'an, even paper with any of its verses, must be treated with external and spiritual reverence. Islamic mystical writing is mostly from Sufism (from *suf* – wool worn in imitation of monks). The golden age of Muslim mysticism was 750-950 CE. An Islamic truth much emphasised in the Sufi tradition is a sense of the presence of God. In the Qur'an 2:186 we read: 'When my servants question you about Me, tell them that I am near.' Traditional Islam spoke about the great mercy of Allah, but in the mystical tradition especially there is a strong emphasis on God's love and on the devout person responding to that love. One of the greatest proponents of pure love for God was Rabi'a al-Adawiyya (713-801 CE). She was sold as a slave; later she obtained her freedom and went into the desert near Basra where disciples formed around her. Accounts of her sayings and actions, and of her prayers, show her seeking a very pure love for God, with no selfishness. One of her prayers:

> O my God, whatever share of this world you have given me, give it to your enemies, and whatever share of the next world you have given me, give it to my friends. You are enough for me.

Again,

> O my God, my work and my desire in all the world is recollection of you, and in the after world meeting with you. This is what is mine – you do as you will.

A frequently recounted incident:

> One day some friends-of-God saw Rabi'a running with fire in one hand and water in the other. 'Lady of the next world, where are you going and what does this mean?' Rabi'a replied: 'I am going to burn paradise and douse hell-fire, so that both veils may be lifted from those on the quest and they will become sincere of purpose. God's servants will learn to see Him without hope for reward or fear of punishment. As it is now, if you took away hope for reward and fear of punishment, no one would obey or worship.[26]

Such pure love of God will be found only in the greatest mystics of any tradition.

Another of the mystics of Islam was the scholar Abu Hamid Al-Ghazali (1058-1111) who describes a process of *dhikir* or remembrance and reflection:

> Let him reduce his heart to a state in which the existence of anything and its non-existence are the same to him. Then let him sit alone in some corner, limiting his religious duties to what is absolutely necessary, and not occupying himself either with reciting the Koran or considering its meaning or with books of religious traditions or with anything of the sort. And let him see to it that nothing save God most High enters his mind. Then as he sits in solitude, let him not cease saying continuously with his tongue, 'Allah, Allah,' keeping his thought on it. At last he will reach a state when the motion of his tongue will cease, and it will seem as though the word flowed from it. Let him persevere in this until all trace of motion is removed from his tongue, and he finds his heart persevering with the thought. Let him still persevere until the form of the word, its letters and shape, is removed from his heart, and there remains the idea alone, as clinging to his heart, inseparable from it. So far, all is dependent on his will and choice; but to bring the mercy of God does not stand in his will or choice. He has now laid himself bare to the breathings of that mercy, and nothing remains but to await what God will open to him, as God has done after this manner to prophets and saints. If he follows that course, he may see that the light of the Real will shine out in his heart. At first unstable, like a flash of lightning, it turns and returns; and sometimes it hangs back. And if it returns, sometimes it abides and sometimes it is momentary. And if it abides, sometimes its abiding is long, and sometimes short.[27]

In this text, if the word God were substituted for *Allah*, many experts in spirituality would find it very difficult to guess its provenance.

Finally, we should be aware of differing reactions to mysticism in Islam as in other faith traditions. There have been undoubted errors in the sayings of some mystics. Some would be regarded as unorthodox, and, in certain Moslem quarters, there is a note of caution about mysticism. But religious persons of many faiths will recognise the authenticity and beauty of Islam's finest mystics.

Those who are engaged in interfaith dialogue find that discussion on doctrinal matters is very difficult and rarely fruitful. Discussion on human rights and moral issues can show greater agreement; but it in the area of spirituality and mysticism that the great religions come closest.

New Age 'Mysticism'

At a totally different remove from the supremely disinterested and pure love of the Islamic Rabi'a is the so-called mysticism of New Age. In treating of mysticism as in other areas, New Age shows itself to be radically turned in on the seeker. A major document on the New Age from the Vatican Council for Culture and for Interreligious Dialogue, *Jesus Christ the Bearer of the Water of Life: A Christian reflection on the New Age*, gives a valuable, if rather dense summary of the differences in section 3.4 'Mysticism and the New Age'.

> For Christians, the spiritual life is a relationship with God which gradually through his grace becomes deeper, and in the process also sheds light on our relationship with our fellow men and women, and with the universe. Spirituality in *New Age* terms means experiencing states of consciousness dominated by a sense of harmony and fusion with the Whole. So 'mysticism' refers not to meeting the transcendent God in the fullness of love,

but to the experience engendered by turning in on oneself, an exhilarating sense of being at one with the universe, a sense of letting one's individuality sink into the great ocean of Being.

This fundamental distinction is evident at all levels of comparison between Christian mysticism and *New Age* mysticism. The *New Age* way of purification is based on awareness of unease or alienation, which is to be overcome by immersion into the Whole. In order to be converted, a person needs to make use of techniques which lead to the experience of illumination. This transforms a person's consciousness and opens him or her to contact with the divinity, which is understood as the deepest essence of reality.

The techniques and methods offered in this immanentist religious system, which has no concept of God as person, proceed 'from below'. Although they involve a descent into the depths of one's own heart or soul, they constitute an essentially human enterprise on the part of a person who seeks to rise towards divinity by his or her own efforts. It is often an 'ascent' on the level of consciousness to what is understood to be a liberating awareness of 'the god within'. Not everyone has access to these techniques, whose benefits are restricted to a privileged spiritual 'aristocracy'.

The essential element in Christian faith, however, is God's descent towards his creatures, particularly towards the humblest, those who are weakest and least gifted according to the values of the 'world'. There are spiritual techniques which it is useful to learn, but God is able to by-pass them or do without them. A Christian's 'method of getting closer to God is not based on any *technique* in the strict sense of the word. That would contradict the spirit of childhood called for by the Gospel. The heart of genuine Christian mysticism is not technique: it is always a gift of God; and the one who benefits from it knows himself to be unworthy.

For Christians, conversion is turning back to the Father, through the Son, in docility to the power of the Holy Spirit. The more people progress in their relationship with God – which is always and in every way a free gift – the more acute is the need to be converted from sin, spiritual myopia and self-infatuation, all of which obstruct a trusting self-abandonment to God and openness to other men and women.

All meditation techniques need to be purged of presumption and pretentiousness. Christian prayer is not an exercise in self-contemplation, stillness and self-emptying, but a dialogue of love, one which 'implies an attitude of conversion, a flight from 'self' to the 'You' of God'. It leads to an increasingly complete surrender to God's will, whereby we are invited to a deep, genuine solidarity with our brothers and sisters.[28]

In brief: New Age mysticism is turning inwards on oneself rather than communion with God who is 'totally other'. It is fusion with the universe, an ultimate annihilation of the individual in the unity of the whole. Experience of Self is taken to be experience of divinity, so one looks within to discover authentic wisdom, creativity and power.

It will be seen that this Vatican document is negative towards New Age. A full account of the phenomenon is not possible here.[29] Those who are involved in New Age spiritualities will often also be found interested in several therapies and exercises not in themselves objectionable. A problem for Catholics emerges with many of its doctrines and practices that are radically opposed to the Christian gospel. Some few people journey through New Age to a deeper Christian faith. Whilst one would not recommend this route, it can be that New Age can lessen the pull of immediate satisfaction that cripples faith and human maturity. The danger is that one becomes hooked on New Age and its experience without commitment philosophy.

Conclusion

As we have already seen, Christian mystics all have the notion of search, of a knowing-loving, of purification. Each will have his or her own special focus, e.g. the Pseudo-Dionysius (*fl. c.* 500) was very influential for later writers in his treatment of the dark knowledge of God. St Patrick had profound experiences of God's teaching, and of his care; and he responded by utter surrender to the mission to the Irish. St Catherine of Siena (d. 1380) had deep insights into the role of the Holy Spirit and into Jesus shedding his blood for us; St Ignatius Loyola (d. 1556) had profound Trinitarian vision and left to the Church a practical spirituality and a testimony of 'finding God in all things'. St Paul of the Cross (d. 1775) had profound mystical experiences of the passion of Christ. St Thérèse of Lisieux taught about the value of littleness and of the importance of being a profound source of love in the heart of the Church. And there are hundreds more. We take two from sixteenth-century Spain.

St John of the Cross

John was born at Fontiveros in Spain about 1542. He entered the Carmelites and with the permission of his superiors began to live a stricter life. Later he was persuaded by St Teresa to begin, together with some others, the Discalced reform within the Carmelite friars; this cost him much hard work and many trials. He died in Ubeda in 1591, outstanding in holiness and wisdom, to which his many spiritual writings give eloquent witness. After his death the reform he introduced within the friars eventually separated from the Carmelite Order to become the Order of Discalced Carmelite Friars.

His main works are *The Ascent of Mount Carmel* and *The Dark Night of the Soul*, which speak of the journey of healing and purification that is needed for deep union with God. His *Spiritual Canticle* and *The Living Flame* describe the mystical state. His poems are recognised as being among the finest in the Spanish language.

St Teresa of Avila

Teresa was born in Avila in Spain in 1515. She entered the Carmelites and made great progress in the way of perfection and was granted mystical revelations. Wishing to share in the spiritual renewal of the Church of her time, she began to live her religious life more ardently and soon attracted many companions, to whom she was like a mother. She also helped in the reform of the friars, and in this had to endure great trials. She wrote books which are renowned for their depth of doctrine and which showed her own spiritual experiences. She died at Alba in 1582. After her death the reform she began eventually separated from the Carmelite Order to become the Order of Discalced Carmelites. Her main works are her *Life,* an autobiography which tells of the graces that God gave her; *The Way of Perfection*, which is largely a treatise of prayer, with a splendid commentary on the *Our Father*; and *The Interior Castle*, which describes the mystical path from the very beginning of turning to God to the highest states of mystical union.[30]

* *

The mystics continue to speak to us, to challenge and to delight us. They point a way to the deep human fulfilment that is found in the search for God. All the great mystics were also servants of the Church and of the world. They did not withdraw to enjoy God's favour, but as the result of their transformation, they were continual sources of blessing for society.

Notes

1. *Spiritual Theology* (London: Sheed and Ward, 1980, reprint 1995) 122.

2. See the classic E. Underhill, *Mysticism: The Nature and Development of Spiritual Consciousness* (12th ed. reprinted Oxford: Oneworld, 1993). H.D. Egan, *What Are They Saying about Mysticism?* (New York: Paulist, 1982); H.D. Egan, *Christian Mysticism: The Future of a Tradition* (New York: Pueblo, 1984); H.D. Egan, *An Anthology of Christian Mysticism* (Collegeville: Pueblo/Liturgical Press, 1991); W. Johnston, *Mystical Theology: The Science of Love* (London: HarperCollins, 1995); C.P.M. Jones, *Mysticism, Human and Divine* in C. Jones, G. Wainwright and E. Yarnold, *The Study of Spirituality* (London: SPCK, 1986), pp. 17-24; J.A. Wiseman, 'Mysticism' in M. Downey, ed., *The New Dictionary of Catholic Spirituality* (Collegeville: Glazier/Liturgical Press, 1993), pp. 681-692.

3. For scripture see dictionaries e.g. B. Rigaux and P. Grelot, 'Mystery' in X. Léon-Dufour, ed., *Dictionary of Biblical Theology* (London: Chapman, 1973) pp. 374-377.

4. See Egan, *Christian Mysticism 3*.

5. Ibid., 4.

6. *The Inner Eye of Love: Mysticism and Religion* (San Francisco: Harper and Row, 1978) 20.

7. Published 1902 and often reprinted, e.g. London: Longman Green, 1937.

8. Cited here is twelfth edition reprinted Oxford: Oneworld, 1993.

9. Ibid. 126-127.

10. Ibid. 70.

11. Ibid. 83-84.

12. Ibid. 81.

13. Julian of Norwich cited ibid. 90. Cf. 'God can certainly be loved, but not thought. He can be taken and held by love, but not by thought.' *Cloud of Unknowing*, ch. 8; 'The important thing is not to think much, but to love much; and so do what stirs you to love.' Teresa of Avila, 4 *Mansions* 1:7.

14. *Cloud of Unknowing* ch. 6; see also 'It is love alone that can reach God in this life, not knowing.' Ibid. ch. 8.

15. Underhill, *Mysticism* 232-265.

16. Op. cit. 413-443.

17. H. Egan, *Anthology* xiii.

18. H. Egan, *Anthology*, p. 599

19.   'The Spirituality of the Church of the Future' in *Theological Investigations* 20 (London: Darton, Longman and Todd, 1981), pp. 143-153 at 149.

20.   *Spiritual Canticle* stanza 14 and 15 in *Collected Works*. Tr. K. Kavanaugh and O. Rodriguez (Washington DC: Institute of Carmelite Studies, revised ed. 1991), p. 46.

21.   St Augustine, *Confessions* 10:27. Trans. H. Chadwick (Oxford: University Press World Classics, 1991), p. 201. See for other texts Egan, *Anthology*.

22.   *The Spiritual Canticle* 36:5 in *Collected Works*, pp. 611-612.

23.   See P. Barnes, *World Religions*. Into the Classroom (Dublin: Veritas, 2003) pp. 52-72.

24.   See D. Cohn-Sherbok, *Judaism: History, Belief and* Practice (London and New York: Routledge, 2003) pp. 194-209.

25.   Cohn-Sherbok, *Judaism*, p. 202.

26.   M.A. Sells, ed. and tr. *Early Islamic Mysticism*. Classics of Western Spirituality. (New York/Mahwah: Paulist, 1996), pp. 169 and 151.

27.   Cited in R.A. Nicholson, *The Mystics of Islam* (Harmondsworth: Penguin Arkana Books, 1989 from original 1914), pp. 46-48.

28.   London: Catholic Truth Society, 2003. The text is also on the Vatican website. Steps: 1) www.vatican.va; 2) sitemap; 3) Culture, Pontifical Council;' 4) Jesus Christ the Bearer of the Water of Life (2003). The text has an appendix with a useful glossary of New Age terms.

29.   A bit dated, but perhaps still useful, see C. O'Donnell, 'Movements, Non-Christian and New Age' in *Ecclesia: A Theological Encyclopedia of the Church* (Collegeville: Liturgical Press, 1996) 316-318.

30.   These two paragraphs are from the Irish Carmelite site: www.carmelites.ie. Texts of the two mystics can be found on www.carmelites.info.

Select Bibliography

G. Appleton, ed. *The Oxford Book of Prayer* (Oxford: University Press, 1985, 2002).

G. Beckerlegge, *The World Religions Reader* (London: Routledge with The Open University, 1998). Contains some mystical texts from various religions.

D. and L. Cohn-Sherbok, *Jewish and Christian Mysticism: An Introduction* (London: Gracewing/New York: Continuum, 1994). In two equal parts the authors introduce firstly Jewish and then Christian mystics. There is a brief final chapter 'Convergence and Divergence.'

H.D. Egan, *What Are They Saying about Mysticism?* (New York: Paulist, 1982). Short, very informative, but somewhat dense.

H.D. Egan, *An Anthology of Christian Mysticism* (Collegeville: Liturgical Press, 1991). A selection of texts from fifty-five mystical writers from AD 200 to the present day. There is a fine introduction to each mystic.

J.J. Elias, *Islam* (London: Routledge 1999) pp. 52-59

S. Fanning, *Mystics of the Christian Tradition* (London: Routledge 2001). A rich book with extensive coverage and indications for further study.

U. King, *Christian Mystics: Their lives and legacies throughout the Ages* (London: Routledge, 2004). Short biographies of sixty mystics.

R. A. Nicholson, *The Mystics of Islam* (London: Penguin/Arcana Books, 1989, reprinted from 1914).

M.A. Sells, ed. and tr. *Early Islamic Mysticism: Sufi, Qur'an, Mi'raj, Poetic and Theological Writings.* Classics of Western Spirituality (New York: Paulist, 1996). A scholarly introduction with an abundance of wonderful texts.